Making the Grade

✖

To Ray —

Keep up the great leadership
on school-to-work — it does
make a difference!

Josh M____

Making the Grade

How a New Youth Apprenticeship System Can Change Our Schools and Save American Jobs

Governor John R. McKernan, Jr.,
with
Jobs for America's Graduates
and
Jobs for the Future

Foreword by Tom Peters

LITTLE, BROWN AND COMPANY

BOSTON   NEW YORK   TORONTO   LONDON

First Edition

All proceeds from the sale of this book will go to Jobs for America's Graduates, Inc., and the Center for Youth Apprenticeship in Maine.

Library of Congress Cataloging-in-Publication Data

McKernan, John R.
    Making the grade : how a new youth apprenticeship system can change our schools and save American jobs / John R. McKernan, Jr., with Jobs for America's Graduates and Jobs for the Future ; foreword by Tom Peters. — 1st ed.
        p.   cm.
    ISBN 0-316-56224-6
    1. Apprenticeship programs — United States.   I. Jobs for America's Graduates, Inc.   II. Jobs for the Future (Organization)   III. Title.
HD4885.U5M37   1994
331.25'922'0973 — dc20   94-14445

10   9   8   7   6   5   4   3   2   1

RRD–VA

*Published simultaneously in Canada
by Little, Brown & Company (Canada) Limited*

Printed in the United States of America

To my late son, Peter, for teaching me to appreciate
the goodness and potential in each of us
and
to my wife, Olympia Snowe, for encouraging me
to use that appreciation to improve the lives of
America's children

Contents

Foreword by Tom Peters   ix

Acknowledgments   xiii

1 As Goes Maine, So Goes the Nation   1

2 The New World of Work   9

3 The Schools We've Inherited   29

4 The Consequences of Inaction   63

5 A Revolution Is Needed   81

6 What the Competition Is Doing   105

7 The Maine Youth Apprenticeship Program   125

8 Getting Started: Designing a Youth
   Apprenticeship Program in Your Community   161

Epilogue: Why It All Matters   189

Appendix A. Model State Law   201

Appendix B. State of Maine Legislation   215

Appendix C. Sample Task Force Letter   219

Selected Bibliography and Suggested Readings   221

Index   225

Foreword

TOM PETERS

GOVERNOR JOCK McKERNAN of Maine has not just written one more book about educational reform (though we can use all we can get), he has written a manifesto for revolution in human development for the twenty-first-century economy.

Yes, revolution. In an early draft of the book, Chapter 5 was titled "The Solution." Not good enough, McKernan thought. In the final version you'll find "A Revolution Is Needed." Amen.

Governor McKernan (Republican), Secretary of Labor Bob Reich (Democrat), and a host of others confidently — if with a hint of terror in their voices — assert that two-thirds of American employees and would-be employees are not fit for the twenty-first-century economy. McKernan, hardly an alarmist, even wonders if Edward Luttwak's claim, in his book *The Endangered American Dream,* about America falling into third world status may not be totally overblown.

The fact is, as McKernan clearly indicates, we do a pretty good (or maybe even a little better than that) job with the top one-third of our kids — and badly neglect the rest. And while the top third, make no mistake, are vitally important to our future, they are (by definition) far from the whole story of future American economic prowess. (Nor can we ignore the social disarray caused, increasingly, by leaving the majority behind.)

We must face and embrace the new economic truths, McKernan vociferously urges. This doesn't mean that 100 percent of American youngsters need attain four-year (or more) degrees. Truth is, most jobs still don't call for four-year degrees — but they do call for a *solid* K-12 background *and something more.* The something more that McKernan describes, champions, and is experimenting boldly with in Maine is, in his terms, the new youth apprenticeship.

Though McKernan has visited and studied Japanese and European systems extensively, and though he admires the European apprentice model (especially Germany's), this program is unique and all American.

Chapters 7 and 8 get to the heart of the matter — a very nitty-gritty look at Maine's pioneering and sweeping apprenticeship program, followed by an eminently practical, step-by-step guide for getting started anywhere.

The devil *is* in the details, and I can hardly do the Maine program justice in twenty-five words or less. I will say one key is the thirteenth year of work-education (sixteen weeks in the classroom, thirty-four weeks at work), which amounts to a critical post-high-school educational accelerator and, in effect, one-half an associate degree. Another pillar is *very* close coordination between the program's parent, the Maine Youth Apprenticeship Program, and the nuts-and-bolts needs of the local business community — as decided (significantly) by the business community itself. Maine also offers a startling guarantee: if the student is not trained as advertised, the state will pay for retraining.

To get from here to there means waging several battles. One calls for a "profound overhaul" of our current approach to education. McKernan's former commissioner of education, Eve Bither (now at the Department of Education in Washington), has said the schoolroom is "the only place left in America where the relatively young sit and watch the relatively old work." Our passive, pound-in-the-facts-like-rivets approach to education (stolen shamelessly and usefully, for a time, from Henry Ford's production-line model of organization) is antithetical to the need of tomorrow's (today's!) workplace. Wholesale teacher reeducation, then, is near the top of the national needs list.

Parents must shoulder their full share of the blame, too. And I don't just mean broken families, and so forth. McKernan refers to the preponderance of studies (and I've seen a bushel of statistics) that show almost all parents giving the school system D's and F's but giving their kids' schools A's and B's. Come off it, Mom and Dad. The system, including your youngins' school is wounded, maybe mortally — and if you don't get it, and do something about it, who will? This is/ must be your fight, not just Jock McKernan's and his fellow reformers'.

But the biggest battle, says the governor, is with business. To be sure, business has lots of reasons to be skeptical about what it imagines as a bureaucratic, government-administered training program aimed at shoving apprentices down its throat. (And McKernan admits that in the Maine program, many mistakes were made in early efforts to match training and specific, local business needs; the Germans are masters at this matching process, incidentally.) Though the onus may well be on "the bureaucrats" to prove their willingness to listen and engage in a true partnership with business, business must come at least halfway. Urgently.

From the crusty, pragmatic northeast corner of the nation, Governor McKernan says he began "by looking out on the [changing] world from the statehouse, but what I found led me, in the end, back to the school-house." It was an inspirational trip. Or, at least, an inspired beginning. McKernan is also correct, as I see it, when he says that the program (revolution, remember) he recommends is "not just a way of improving education and the workforce; it is a fundamental choice that the United States has to make."

It is revolution. It is a fundamental choice. We've been singing "nation at risk" for a decade or so now. We are at risk. The crisis deepens. The economic and social time bomb ticks. When in the hell are we going to quit piddling and fiddling, tinkering here and there, and put it atop the American agenda?

Acknowledgments

WHEN I FIRST BEGAN WORKING to reform our schools, I had the conventional view that our challenge was to send more students on to college. Like so many others, "college" for me meant the familiar four-year colleges of my own youth.

Over the years, however, my views have changed. Countless businesspeople have told me that American high-school graduates are deficient in the skills employers need. Educators like Frank Newman, president of the Education Commission of the States, convinced me that all students can, in fact, learn. So, yes, more students must go to college. However, it is increasingly clear that *all* of our children must go on to at least *some* level of postsecondary education. Our challenge is to design an educational system that offers a sufficient variety of learning methods so that they have that opportunity. I believe the national youth apprenticeship system I recommend in this book would bring us closer to that goal and, by so doing, also improve the standard of living in America in the twenty-first century.

I want to thank Charlie Hayward, president of Little, Brown and Company, for understanding the importance of the problems facing America and the potential for the solutions suggested in this book. I also want to thank my editor at Little, Brown, Bill Phillips, for his enthusiasm, insights, encouragement, and guidance throughout the preparation of the manuscript; and Steve Schneider for his thoughtful editing.

I deeply appreciate the financial, research, and technical support from the board and staff of Jobs for America's Graduates, Inc. JAG president Ken Smith, in particular, has spent countless hours discussing education and workforce issues with me as my thoughts have evolved; and the JAG students and job specialists are a constant source of inspiration. Likewise, Hilary Pennington, president of Jobs for the Future, and her staff have provided technical support and helped me put in better perspective the school-to-work movement in our country. Both of these organizations provided valuable input; in the end, however, any opinions expressed are mine.

Without the financial support of UNUM and L.L. Bean in Maine, Siemens Corporation, and the Pew Charitable Trust, this project might never have begun; and without the final fact-checking by Kathy Dalle-Molle, it might never have been completed!

I am particularly indebted to Donna Sammons Carpenter for her wordsmithing and the improvements she has made in the original text. Her efforts and those of Richard Lourie, Erik Hansen, Sebastian Stuart, Charles Simmons, and Jozefa Stuart have made for a much more readable book.

Finally, I want to thank my friends and staff for their support, advice, and time: Dave Lackey for his extra effort in helping with the rewrites and editing; John Fitzsimmons for synthesizing the lessons learned from our own program; Cyndi Fortier for once again organizing my efforts; my wife, Olympia Snowe, Bob Moore, Sharon and Dan Miller, Jean Mattimore, Susan Brown, Bill Cassidy, Leo Martin, Chris Lyons, Susan Shows, Carolyn Warner, and Chris Perry for their constructive suggestions; and Rosemarie Smith with the help of Marianne MacMaster for actually getting the printed words on the page.

Most of all, I want to thank the parents, students, teachers, principals, superintendents, and businesses who took the risk to begin the program in our state. You are the pioneers, and America is the beneficiary.

1

As Goes Maine,
So Goes the Nation

M AINE AND ITS PEOPLE keep you honest.
With its glacial boulders, rugged Atlantic coast,
vast forests, and deep white winters, Maine encourages
clear thinking. Its citizens enjoy a worldwide reputation
for integrity, common sense, and a strong work ethic.

I was born and bred in Maine, and in 1986, at
the age of thirty-seven, I announced my candidacy for
governor. I offered my assessment of the state, what I
hoped the future would bring, and what I would do to
realize those hopes. I won; and at my inauguration, the
ceremony had to be delayed for almost an hour because
of traffic jams. People came in droves to behold that
wonder: Maine's first Republican governor in twenty
years.

It was a good start, one buoyed by the economy's
upsurge in the 1980s. During my first term, Maine enjoyed greater prosperity than it had ever known. Then
came the 1990s, and things changed. The first sign was
a drop in sales tax revenues, followed by a decline in

state income tax revenues. Other indicators quickly followed: layoffs, closings, plywood on windows. The recession that would soon hit the rest of the United States — and affect the whole world — had come to Maine.

Businesses that fail or move to where labor is cheaper are more than just economic indicators for a specific region — they are indicators of lost jobs for the individual. When the economy changed, many Mainers were suddenly out of work. Firms left or went out of business: Emple Knitting Mills closed, the Timberland Shoe Company moved out of the state, Mecon Manufacturing, which produces circuit breakers, shifted its operations to the Caribbean.

As unemployment statistics rolled into my office, I looked around the country and found that Maine was not alone. I soon realized that the recession had been bad enough, but even the recovery would bring a slowing of job creation. In this new global economic competition, good jobs in America would be harder and harder to find. Because many of Maine's companies were involved in more traditional industries, we were seeing the phenomenon first, but the rest of the nation was right behind us. Unfortunately, we were once again demonstrating a familiar old saying: As goes Maine, so goes the nation.

Though U.S. workers are more productive than their overseas counterparts, there is such a discrepancy in wages (the average hourly manufacturing wage — including benefits — is $15.45 in the United States, $2.17 in Mexico, sixty-eight cents in Thailand, and an astonishing twenty-five cents in China) that, even with added transportation costs, it's often cheaper to move jobs abroad.

But low wages are only a part of the problem. Jobs are also moving to foreign countries because the technological skills of the workforce in those countries are demonstrably higher. This is happening throughout the United States, and the major reason is that our workforce has not been trained to do the jobs that modern technology demands. We are not competing only against lower wages, but also against more highly skilled labor in countries like Japan and Germany. If other countries can produce a labor force trained in modern technology, why can't we?

In 1991, I heard economist and present secretary of labor Robert Reich say something that I have not forgotten. Today, he said, money can be moved anywhere in the world, and so can technology and managers. He concluded by stating that "the determining factor for America in the new global economic competition will be the skill of our workforce."

Competition in the new global economy is a national problem that affects each one of our communities. Across the United States we are losing jobs to countries that can supply U.S. companies with the skilled workers they need. Yes, the lack of trained workers is losing us jobs, but, just as serious, it is also eroding our edge in the competition for world markets.

Total quality management, work redesign, process reengineering — these are the buzzwords for today's cost-cutting techniques. Whatever it is called, companies willing to commit to these new approaches find that they keep making quantum improvements in productivity. Consequently, they need a smaller workforce, one that is trained in the skills needed for today's electronic technology. Companies may begin by targeting work, but inevitably they end by targeting workers — for layoffs. The result is unemployment.

Minnesota-based 3M Corporation, to mention only one example among many, originally set up a software-writing operation in Bangalore, India, because of the availability of trained technicians and managers. They followed this with a manufacturing unit, which now employs 120 people to make electrical connectors, chemicals, and pressure-sensitive tapes.

John Naisbitt predicted this trend in his 1982 book, *Megatrends,* where he asked, "Jobs will be available, but who will possess the high-tech skills to fill them?" That question remains as valid today, more than a decade later. The United States has yet to commit itself to policies that will allow us to answer, "U.S. workers will have those skills!"

As I have looked at the education system in our country, I have come to realize that we are seriously shortchanging our children. With our present approach to schooling, we are depriving them of a secure future because we are not giving them the skills to compete in the current global economy. It is not the young people who are failing; we have failed them. We are losing a whole generation of U.S. children because our schools have neglected to prepare them for the complex demands of today's marketplace.

The very nature of jobs has changed in this technological age. People who want good jobs today need markedly different skills than those who once depended on the telephone or the typewriter. This is especially true of the frontline worker in the labor market. The old assembly line jobs are largely gone. Companies today are looking for team workers, men and women who can handle a lot of information and then make intelligent decisions as part of a group effort. This future workforce demands a different kind of education. An army wouldn't get far without noncoms and privates; a company cannot hope to be productive without a competent, skilled workforce to build on.

Until we get to the root of the problem in our educational system, we will see neighbors, friends, and families suffer, whether in the state of Maine or in the rest of the country. In this era of globalization, we cannot lose sight of the needs of our national economy — and that means making investments to benefit our own in this changed world.

I remember something Stephen Barley of Cornell University's School of Labor Relations once said: "Once you're able to automate all the control systems in the manufacturing operation, you don't need many operatives any more. What you need are technicians who can keep the integrated manufacturing systems running. . . . Conceivably this might mean that firms would gut the unskilled workforce and just leave top management and technicians."

Certain things have become clear to me, both about Maine and the country as a whole. There is now a true world economy, and everything from shirts to software will go where the costs are low and the workers are well trained. After the North American Free Trade Agreement (NAFTA) and the recent accords on the General Agreement on Tariffs and Trade (GATT), this trend will quicken. So, if the future here at home does indeed belong to upper management and well-trained technicians, then the quality of that future for the United States depends on the quality of the education we offer our citizens. (There are, of course, self-taught technicians and self-made executives — a great U.S. tradition of mavericks and outsiders that I hope will continue to feed and stimulate us for generations to come. But for most of us, formal training is critical.)

When the recession first hit Maine, it was difficult to sort out cause and effect. As a governor, I was able to accumulate a lot of information on the state of the economy, but the trick was how to put it all together.

I could see that ensuring a growing and lasting prosperity would — more than ever before in our nation's history — be a direct function of schooling. A purely academic education was not enough to prepare most of our students. Our children need a gradual introduction to the complexities of the marketplace; and they should be exposed, as early as possible, to on-the-job training. Could we, I asked myself, take our vocational training programs and expand them to meet the challenges of the 1990s? Could we establish, here in the United States, a method by which students can both learn and do at the same time? What we lack is a policy of making education relevant to students by letting them serve as apprentices in the workplace. Why shouldn't students familiarize themselves, both outside and inside the schoolroom, with today's technology?

The philosopher's old wisdom that "knowledge is power," once believed by only a few, is proven true by the new economic realities. I am convinced we must embrace that truth; facing it is inevitable. The answer to our economic problems lies in education, in the proper preparation and training of our young people. But that simple and even obvious answer raises new questions:

- What exactly is the best way to prepare the coming generations?
- What should the roles of government, business, and education be in any reform of our schools?
- How much of the fault lies in our schools?

While pondering these questions, I had to admit to a nagging doubt: Did anything really need to be done? Wouldn't things get back on keel and pretty much take care of themselves as they always had in the past? I have become convinced they won't. This was a hard fact to face, but the United States has always succeeded because it could face hard facts and has been blessed with the ingenuity to find solutions.

I believe America is still blessed with that ingenuity, and that when presented with the facts, we as Americans will act.

2

The New World of Work

People who were born at the beginning of this century probably have seen more change in their lifetime than anyone is ever likely to see again. They grew up in a world where the horse and buggy were still commonplace and electricity a rarity, and they ended their days having seen a man on the moon and the rise to dominance of television and the computer.

Current changes are perhaps not as dramatic as those that preceded them, but they are equally unsettling, and their impact will be felt for decades to come. Earlier in the century labor was transformed as the United States went from being an agrarian society to an industrial giant. And yet for all the difference between working on the land and on the assembly line, both farm and factory shared a certain similarity: the work was composed fundamentally of a series of tasks endlessly repeated.

The industrial society was based on a system of

mass manufacturing developed early in the twentieth century. Complex jobs were broken down into a myriad of simple rote tasks, which the worker repeated with machinelike efficiency. Educated planners and supervisors managed the system. They planned company strategy, they implemented changes, they motivated workers, and they solved problems. Carefully set up administrative procedures allowed management to keep control of a large number of workers. Under this system, most employees did not need to be educated. It was far more important that they be reliable, steady, and willing to follow directions.

Manufacturing methods like these are still used to produce a high volume of inexpensive goods and services. But they don't work in the present-day market, which demands quality, variety, and responsiveness to consumer tastes. Mixing the old with the new, installing complex new technologies without changing administrative methods, burdens companies with a cumbersome and inefficient managerial bureaucracy.

In our time, the very nature of human labor has undergone a profound transformation, one that history may show to be every bit as significant as the technological revolution our grandparents witnessed.

Political changes of immense importance also took place in the last half of the twentieth century. Europe's empires collapsed, and the United States emerged as the leading world power. For some fifty years the United States and the Soviet Union were locked in a nuclear standoff. No one predicted the sudden collapse of Soviet communism and the Soviet empire. No one foresaw the abrupt transformation of the other communist giant, China, into a strange hybrid of one-party tyranny and unbridled capitalist growth.

Now, as the century closes, we find ourselves in a period of turbulent transition toward a global economy and worldwide economic competition. There are already those who feel nostalgia for the moral and political certainties of the cold war, but that world now belongs to history every bit as much as Britannia, the empire that once ruled the waves.

As Tom Peters says in his book *Thriving on Chaos,* "All organizations must now be jerked rapidly in new directions. Moreover, the requisite change in direction is taking place against a backdrop of ever more confusing messages from the environment — cut costs but achieve better quality; decentralize and recentralize. Even if conventional planning tools were once effective as direction centers (a questionable assertion), they are much too slow — and not blunt enough — for today's needs."

President Bush coined the term "new world order" for the post–cold war world. The irony of the term, which is now universally used, is that the one thing conspicuously lacking in the new world is order. The tendency so far has been toward disintegration, with Yugoslavia as the most obvious and tragic example. What does distinguish the new landscape is the absence, between great powers, of any intense political rivalries that imminently could lead to war. In fact, political competition seems to have been replaced by economic competition. These changes may not be as epic as the developments our elders witnessed, but they are, in their own way, even more radical.

Though it may not be orderly, we do have a new economic world order. And, as one of the characters in Michael Crichton's novel on Japanese-American commercial relations, *Rising Sun,* remarks, "Business is war." That may be too strong a statement, but there is no question that the competition for the world's wealth is now wide open and being fought in dead earnest. The victors will emerge enriched and the losers impoverished. The casualties will not be in lives but in quality of life.

The new world of work and the new economic world order are very closely related. Some have expressed the opinion that the great new force of our times — technology — was partially responsible for the collapse of the Soviet Union. Information, which is the lifeblood of current technology, could not circulate freely in a society ruled by political censorship. To remedy this, Mikhail Gorbachev introduced his policy of openness, glasnost. But it turns out that once information begins to circulate freely, behavior changes. People will no longer put up with the intolerable and will begin to demand what all people want, a good life with a proper mix of prosperity, security, and liberty.

Technology has revolutionized our times and the nature of work. In some ways, it has humanized labor by freeing people from the mechanical and the repetitive. But it is also unrelenting in its demand for trained intelligence. The type of intelligence required by agriculture — and it's easy to forget how much knowledge a farmer must possess — was not of the kind learned in school. The same is true of those who worked in industry. The U.S. tinker-and-fix-it mentality always came into play when there were glitches on the line. But those skills were usually learned through experimentation done in the garage or the basement, not through formal learning.

Farmers, once some 80 percent of the population, are now 5 percent. The industrial jobs of the past are disappearing just as precipitately. The U.S. worker's future is not on the assembly line. From now on, job growth will be in professional, technical, and sales fields, requiring the highest education and the best-honed skills. Forty percent of today's jobs are in low-skill occupations; by the year 2000, only 27 percent will be. In that same period, high-skill jobs will rise from 24 percent to 41 percent. Since the 1980s, competition in the world market has increased to such an extent that U.S. business can no longer compete if it has to rely on low-skilled workers.

Lean Production

Once again the shape of the working nation is undergoing a drastic change. One of the first victims of the new economic order was Henry Ford's invention, which had launched the manufacturing revolution in the first place: the assembly line. That basic prototype, which could produce cars or televisions, bombs or blankets, is quickly being replaced by a new shape — not by a production line and a ladder of authority, but by interactive teams whose responsibilities and authority respond to the pace and demands of the work itself.

To describe this new pattern of labor, James

Womack, coauthor of *The Machine That Changed the World,* coined the phrase "lean production." At Japanese auto firms, Womack and his colleagues noticed a dramatic difference in productivity. Whereas the assembly line emphasized an endless division of labor, breaking it down into the simplest units possible, lean production relies on teamwork in which autonomous groups perform a designated set of tasks. Rather than forcing men and women to spend their working lives tightening the same bolt over and over again, the new workplace demands that they continually learn new skills.

For the lean producer, employees are the most important asset. They are valuable because the flow of feedback that can result in improvements of production design is too valuable to be bottled up in a vertical hierarchy. As Robert Reich wrote in his article "Education and the Next Economy":

> Much of the relevant information lies below — among production workers, production engineers, salespeople and others in direct contact with suppliers, production processes, and customers. There is not enough time for all the relevant information to be passed upward to the top decision makers and then down again in the form of new operating instructions. With valuable information and expertise dispersed throughout the organization, top managers cannot hope to solve problems and provide answers; their jobs must be to create environments in which people can identify and solve problems for themselves.

In fact, Reich is saying that in our new world of work, the old line between management and labor has been swept aside by a torrent of information. This information is so vital to a company's survival that it can ill afford to ignore the sources that supply it. In the modern context, *value added* means *intelligence added* — and the best intelligence comes from the best information, which often lies with labor. This same force has also blurred the traditional line between goods and services so that, as Reich puts it, there is "no longer any meaningful distinction between the two categories."

Where massive runs of standardized products with long lives once brought in high profits, the new marketplace, with its educated consumer, requires an ever-growing variety. As a result, the life of a product is shortened and production volume per product falls.

No longer can we expect to lead our competitors by simply producing more of the same at lower cost. To regain a competitive advantage, the United States must shift toward work with value based on quality, flexibility, precision, and specialization. Low costs alone are not the answer. High quality at the lowest possible cost is the answer.

According to Womack, one of the tenets of lean production posits perfection as a goal. This concept is in direct contrast to the mass producer's goal of "good enough." When defects in design and production are tolerated, they tend to happen regularly and to be accepted by everyone in an organization. Though creating a perfect product every time is obviously an impossible achievement by anyone anywhere, the belief that this goal can be reached eventually, through hard work and constant and continual improvement, sends the lean producer down a decidedly different and better path than the now outmoded mass producer.

Reengineering

Michael Hammer and James Champy, in their book *Reengineering the Corporation,* have created terms that define these new ways of working. According to them, "Work units change — from functional departments to process teams." These units are composed of people who naturally belong together to complete a piece of work, from its beginning to its conclusion. The focus here is on the job to be completed, not on maintaining a hierarchy of departments to maintain quality control over the work being done by the men and women in the trenches.

What that means in practice was described in "America's Choice: High Skills or Low Wages," published by the National Center on Education and the Economy in 1990.

It seems that in 1984 just about nothing was going right at an IBM circuit board manufacturing plant in Austin, Texas. Processes were slow, costs were high, there was a lot of waste, both of time and materials. In fact, IBM executives complained that they could save tens of millions of dollars buying the boards from outside suppliers. Most companies would have simply shut down the plant, but IBM, wanting to keep as many people as possible working, was loath to take such a drastic step. It decided to give the plant a clear mandate for change.

Perhaps the most glaring problem was the plant's enormous indirect costs. For every one worker actually assembling the circuit boards, there were two workers inspecting, repairing, transporting, keeping machines up, scheduling, and supervising. In spite of all this padding, defective boards were being shipped, and expensive inventory sat idle.

Management saw work teams as the answer. Teams with the skills needed to tackle the whole process. Instead of do-your-job-and-pass-it-on, each team member became responsible for their circuit boards from initial parts ordering through final inspection. Workers who had previously spent all day scheduling, for example, were now part of the actual production team. The ratio of indirect to hands-on workers dropped to less than one to one.

Skills became paramount. Old job titles were thrown out and seven levels of manufacturing technical associates (MTAs) were created. Each successive level requires more advanced skills. Previously, a worker would hit a brick career wall after five years. Now, advancement can continue for up to twenty years, as the employee continues to grow and learn.

Imagine what it must feel like to an employee who has been doing a tedious (or even not so tedious), repetitive job day in and day out for years, to suddenly be handed real responsibility, real initiative, real trust. Vera Sharbonez is one such worker. Vera had been feeding circuit boards into a machine for fifteen years, practically since the day she finished high school. The machine would quickly fit each board with transistors and capacitors, Vera would pull it out, inspect it, and put it in the "pass" or "reject" pile. For $10 an hour Vera did this some 1,200 times a day. Pretty numbing stuff.

But decent jobs don't grow on trees, so when Vera got wind of troubles at the plant, she grew nervous. And her fears were only partially assuaged when the MTA system was put into place and she was assigned to a team. She was anxious as to whether she could perform her added tasks, and suspicious that the company was trying to get more work for the same pay.

Slowly, however, things took shape. Vera learned to set up her machine in the morning and fix it when it broke down. She and her team members started setting their own schedules and assuming full responsibility for meeting them. Team leadership alternated among members. This truly was the new world of work.

IBM didn't just toss its workers into the deep end and hope they knew how to swim; it set up a comprehensive education and training program. Continual learning is now the order of the day — more than 5 percent of the plant's payroll is spent keeping workers up to date on everything they need to know to keep things humming. And often, this process has meant starting with the basics; some workers hadn't finished high school and lacked the reading and math foundation necessary to move on to more advanced learning. But the commitment was there on both sides, and the results have been gratifying.

Every morning when they arrive at the plant, Vera and her teammates sit down and talk about what they're going to accomplish that day. They deal with the storeroom, with suppliers, with customers, they make decisions, they set and meet quality standards. The ball is in their court and they play it. Does Vera still load boards? Yes, but only about 25 percent of the time.

And the change hasn't been limited to the team level. Workers have a voice in plant investment and design decisions, they've learned to study options, to understand cost/benefit analysis — in short, to see themselves as part of an integrated whole.

Workers like Vera Sharbonez have met the challenge. Yes, the work is often harder, the responsibility greater, but so is the respect earned. Vera even claims, only half jokingly, that she and her team could run the plant now.

The bottom line? Productivity is up 200 percent, quality has improved fivefold, inventory is down 40 percent. There have been no layoffs. And IBM's management has wisely not frozen the changes; they understand that only by staying fluid and evolving, by listening to their workers and giving them even more responsibility and trust, will the bottom line stay healthy.

Vera is one of the fortunate ones. Her plant was farsighted enough to adapt to the changing world of work. And she and her coworkers were fortunate that IBM was willing to absorb the expense of retraining them.

But more than education and skills are required by this revolutionized world. Since rapid and relentless change is part of the very nature of the new technology, the new worker must also be able to adapt. It has been estimated that soon people can expect to change careers three or four times in the course of their working lives. That in turn means that the best-adapted worker is the one not only possessing a specific set of skills, but the one who is able to acquire new ones as needed.

While thinking about how to prepare young people for this new world of work, I spent some time with Frank Doyle, executive vice president of General Electric, and, in my opinion, one of the best thinkers on the future of the U.S. workforce.

GE is one of the few "name brand" companies that emerged from the 1980s stronger than it began the decade. It is consistently ranked by chief executive officers and those who study corporations as perhaps the best-managed and best-organized company in the world. Yet Doyle believes that the successes of the 1980s were much easier than the challenges of the 1990s.

"It didn't take long to realize that in order to assure our being competitive, we had to close plants and release thousands of excess workers to keep costs in line, while consistently striving to improve quality and reduce cycle time."

The critical challenge in the 1990s, maintains Doyle, will be how to best use "people power." The corporate winners will be those that know how to effectively organize, train, and apply the skills of their people on a highly flexible and efficient basis. Productivity improvements of 5 to 7 percent annually require this, not just more capital or technology.

That challenge, in the words of Doyle, is GE's "next act": putting in place systems so that GE will be second to none wherever it decides to compete.

These are lofty goals — yet based on the confidence

and the conviction of a company that has met the challenge of the 1980s and has a clear vision of what is needed in the 1990s.

Ask anyone the top five things they associate with Maine, and internationally known clothing retailer L.L. Bean is sure to be on the list. The company has a well-deserved reputation for selling superior goods at a reasonable price. It also has $850 million in annual sales, 85 percent of it generated by its famous catalogs. So when the catalogs department had problems, Leon Gorman, president of L.L. Bean, was quick to act.

An outdated production process, which often resulted in large cost overruns due to rework, overtime, and late fees, was causing morale to sag. The creative team responsible for the beloved catalogs simply couldn't keep up with the company's burgeoning growth and skyrocketing circulation.

Management studied the problem, and once again the solution turned out to be a more horizontal work flow based on cross-functional teams. When production was streamlined and rework virtually eliminated, it became obvious that a vastly more sophisticated computer system was needed. One improvement snowballed right into the next. Morale went through the roof as employees realized they were being supported, being given the tools they needed to do the great job they wanted to do. There was a lot of training involved to get the hang of the advanced systems, but few complaints because the common goal was stressed.

Again, let's cut to the all-important bottom line. L.L. Bean has saved $750,000 in production costs and

$500,000 in returned catalogs annually. And the time it takes to produce a catalog has been reduced by almost a month!

The L.L. Bean example demonstrates how not only the world of work but the world of the individual worker has changed.

Since required skills keep changing, smart employers are more likely to focus on workers' ability to change rather than on any particular skill. The emphasis is put not on what they can do, but on how well they can learn something new. An example from *Reengineering the Corporation* illustrates this nicely:

> Hill's Pet Products, a subsidiary of Colgate-Palmolive, recently built a new plant in Richmond, Indiana, at which the company has implemented many of the principles of reengineered processes. The company's management knew the kind of people they needed to work on the plant floor and set out to hire 150 of them. The company received thousands of applications and the personnel department looked closely at 3,000. When the finalists were selected, practically all of them shared one characteristic: They lacked factory work experience. The applicants who the company wanted mostly turned out to be former schoolteachers, police officers, and others who had the right character and the right education although they lacked factory skills. But that ostensible deficit wasn't a major problem. The company was able

to train the new hires, because these were people who already knew how to learn. . . .

In an environment of flexibility and change, it is clearly impossible to hire people who already know everything they're ever going to need to know, so continuing education over the lifetime of a job becomes the norm in a reengineered company.

To compete in terms of quality instead of cost means to compete with intelligence. But intelligence has no value unless it is trained. Training is another word for education. For that reason, education has now become crucial to our nation's economic health and well-being.

I've mentioned earlier how the agricultural workforce of this country has been reduced. Industry took 82 percent of our nation away from the land. They weren't needed there any longer. They moved to the cities and worked in factories. But currently only about 17 percent of our workforce is directly involved in manufacturing. Attrition, obsolescence, and new technology have wiped out those jobs. Still, as we have seen, technology not only eliminates jobs — it also creates new ones. Just as men and women who once worked the land found other jobs, those who once worked on the assembly line are finding other jobs. (The food industry still employs about one in four Americans. Is this a contradiction? No. Because the farmers and ranchers who grow, tend, and harvest our food see a small fraction of the billions we spend at the checkout counter. Most of it goes to the people on either side of the food chain — the bankers, commodity traders, chemical companies, packers, shippers, and retailers. In 1900 this was not the case — people didn't go out Friday night for pizza, and they didn't throw a lasagna into the microwave.)

It used to be that someone — anyone — with a small amount of training could become a bank teller. Basic math skills and the ability to deal with the public were the primary requirements. The advent of the Automated Teller Machine (ATM) has all but made that job as outmoded as the pony express rider's. In and of itself, that's not such bad news. Though there's no longer much demand for tellers, there is a huge demand for technicians to service these machines.

Some critics of our economy and educational system say we're preparing too many of our students to work at McDonald's or Wendy's — honest work, of course, but no one's ultimate dream career. Though they may sound like pessimists, these critics may soon prove to have taken too rosy a view. Though the fast food industry is now among the country's largest employers, automation technology has even begun cutting away at this last refuge for untrained workers. This automation has already been launched and in the not-too-distant future will be commonplace. Customers will punch in their own orders; laser cookers and automatic retrieval systems will do the rest. Nearly all payment will be automated by machines accepting credit cards, bank cards, and cash.

In his article "Future Workplace Is Shocking," Dr.

William Daggett, director of the International Center for Leadership in Schenectady, New York, tells a story that, though only anecdotal, still rings true:

> I recently met a 23-year-old who had bought a house from a chemical engineer who worked for the General Electric company. I mention that it was a chemical engineer . . . because the guy made pretty good money. He and his wife moved to a new community and sold their house to this 23-year-old who earns enough money to live in that house. He had no family income behind him, did not have a day of post-secondary education, and doesn't speak English very well. He's a German whom the local fast-food restaurant hired to run the high-speed laser cooker. What happens when the high-speed laser cooker shuts down? They're out of business, aren't they? Like the bank. Do you know what they pay the German to run that high-speed laser cooker system? They pay him $29.50 an hour. This young man has a 24-year-old friend who shares that responsibility with him. She doesn't speak English very well, either. She's from Japan. . . .

I once heard a futurist say that we ought not to worry about becoming a nation of fast food counter clerks because in the future those jobs will be done by robots. The jobs, he went on to say, will be in the countries that make robots.

Technology has altered the shape of the economy from top to bottom, from boardroom to burger grill.

This new sense of how tasks should be delegated and performed has spread, blurring the distinctions between management and labor, as well as between goods and services; but it has created one especially sharp distinction — between those who possess the new skills and those who don't. That distinction spells economic survival for each of us.

3

The Schools We've Inherited

NOT ALL THAT LONG AGO the public school was the pride of the community. Like the town hall, the bank, and the church, it was a serious and important place. Whether made of brick in Boston or stucco in San Francisco, a public school was well constructed and well maintained — civic pride as architecture.

Surrounded by trees and playing fields, schools were visible symbols of a prosperous society passing on to the next generation that most precious gift: education, to both prepare and protect its youth.

All that has changed. Our schools no longer prepare our children to meet the demands of the world they will face when they graduate. (In fact, some schools have become the stage on which society's worst ills are played out.) Schools no longer educate young people; they send them out into the marketplace ill equipped to earn a living in a technological society. Schools are failing in their most important task.

How did this happen? And so fast? The short answer is this: the world changed and our schools didn't. But the short answer doesn't tell us enough.

In what now seems a golden age, the U.S. school system did its job and did it well. It taught the basic skills and turned out good citizens. It was a workshop that took in the children of immigrants and turned out Americans.

Education was the ladder out of poverty for many immigrants, and a mastery of good English was essential. Parents worked hard so that their children could do better than they had done. We have to beware of idealizing the past, but neither should we forget that the American dream did indeed reflect reality — in many families, each generation exceeded the success of the preceding one.

The New England mind shaped our school system. Many of our early schools were built in New England, and very good schools they were, from first grade all the way up to universities like Harvard and Yale (and smaller colleges like my alma mater, Dartmouth College, and two-hundred-year-old Bowdoin College in Maine). As the United States spread west, settlements were founded. Schools were fashioned on the New England model, and New England–trained educators came to teach in them. The essentials were reading, writing, and arithmetic — the three R's. Kids whose parents came from the Rhineland or County Kildare, Bialystok or the Mezzogiorno, began each day by pledging allegiance to the flag of their new country and then learned its history, not as a succession of dates but as an inspiring tale of success. They read the great documents of U.S. history from the Declaration of Independence and the Bill of Rights to Abraham Lincoln's Gettysburg Address. They memorized "O Captain, My Captain," which Walt Whitman wrote commemorating Lincoln's assassination.

Students learned about the Industrial Revolution; though it started in England, it soon took root in the United States, where important industrial machinery was invented — from the cotton gin to the light bulb, the phonograph to the Model T. U.S. history was taught not just to educate the students but also to instill in them a sense of pride, optimism, and ambition. The United States was the land of opportunity, and its history proved it.

In the late nineteenth and early twentieth centuries, most of the nation's high schools were roughly uniform in quality (except in the South, where white schools were markedly superior to black schools), and they served several generations well. No schools, however, placed much emphasis on the specific skills valued in the world of work. There was a good reason for this attitude. Young people who were going to work on the farm or on an assembly line didn't need to be taught much in the way of advanced vocational or educational skills.

That began to change early in the twentieth century when business and public policy officials began to worry about the lack of trade skills among children coming out of school. Junior high schools were added to grammar schools to lengthen school attendance, and vocational high schools were established in some areas.

Some of these programs worked well in preparing

young people for work. Students got to smell hot steel or wood shavings. They learned their way around a lathe and a metal cutter. Those who took auto shop were ready to get under a hood and go to work the day they graduated. For some graduates it was just a matter of turning a part-time job into a full-time one.

But nearly from the start vocational teaching had some serious flaws. The courses were often inadequate, the material outdated. In Michigan, high-school printing classes in the 1930s trained students to set type by hand, despite the fact that Linotype and Monotype machines were used in printing shops. Some Midwestern high schools were still teaching blacksmithing when there were thirty million cars on U.S. roads.

It didn't seem to matter that much. Industry had already settled on a design for factory work — a series of simple, repetitive tasks that could be learned quickly and performed by relatively unskilled workers. The Ford Motor Company assembly lines in Dearborn, Michigan, were the purest expression of the idea and became the model for industry the world over.

Industrial labor could be mind-numbing or back-breaking, but it was considered honest work, it was respected, and it was often steady. It was clear to everyone that the United States owed its wealth to industry. An industrial nation had to value its workers, although the unions still had to fight hard for improved wages and working conditions.

Industrial workers had their pride and were also buoyed by the belief that their children would lead better lives — attaining a better education, a better income, and more dignified work. They knew that, barring war or economic depression, there was a good chance that would come true. The motto was always "onward and upward."

The accepted way up was education. The high-school diploma was a passport to opportunity. This was true even throughout the Great Depression. The great change came in the 1950s; expectations rose, but so did educational requirements.

In the nineteenth century and the first half of this century, sending children to college was largely the prerogative of the upper class. In 1940, only 4.6 percent of U.S. citizens over age twenty-five had a college degree.

The prosperity of the 1950s was a major factor in changing a privilege into a common aspiration, but there were other factors. World War II, which had made the United States a world leader, had also exposed young Americans to the cultures of other countries. The GI Bill enabled working-class youngsters to go to college, so that by the end of the decade, the percentage of U.S. college graduates had almost doubled. In the 1960s, the number more than doubled again. By 1990, college and university enrollment was up to 13.5 million. The college degree was now what the high-school diploma had once been.

What was expected of the college graduate? In the nineteenth and early twentieth centuries, an educated person knew Latin and some Greek, had read the classics of Western literature, and was familiar with the principles of mathematics, the sciences, philosophy, and theology. Public schools produced citizens; universities created the cultured class.

It took the cold war for our society to make higher

education respond to reality. In 1957, Sputnik I and Sputnik II went up, shocking the United States. The communists were winning in space. Not everyone remembers this now, but I remember growing up during the early space race, when the United States seemed to be constantly behind. The Soviets sent up the first satellites, the first dog, the first man, and the first woman. U.S. rockets reportedly misfired. There was a sense of national embarrassment.

The response was a federally funded push for more physicists and engineers. And by the end of the 1960s, it was the flag of the United States of America that waved proudly on the moon.

That was a solemn and momentous victory for this country. And it also provides us with a good example of society pulling together and aligning education with national purpose.

The idea that education should be "relevant" gained increasing currency in the turbulence of the 1960s, when a generation felt the need to address social issues. The number of degrees granted in sociology and psychology jumped by more than thirty thousand a year between 1966 and 1970.

But it is not only the tastes and motivations of young Americans that have changed over the last thirty-odd years. The period between the 1960s and the 1990s also saw the rise of intense international competition. "Made in Japan" went from being a joke to a warning. Emerging from the rubble of World War II, Germany performed its economic miracle, the *Wirtschaftswunder*.

Learning the lessons of World War I, which had left Germany wounded and dangerous, we helped our former enemies rebuild their countries after World War II. The United States acted generously and sensibly, but with a somewhat ironic result. Germany and Japan were rebuilt from bombed-out ruins, whereas the United States, undamaged by the war, was left with outdated plants and aging machinery. Prohibited from keeping large military arsenals, Germany and Japan were spared their expense. But it was not only these paradoxical advantages of defeat that eventually made these countries our rivals in trade — it was the fact that their labor force was becoming better trained through the integration of business and education.

A Question of Competence

Bearing this in mind, some U.S. companies went global and made their products wherever they could find a trained labor pool at low wages; other corporations bet on high-tech streamlining at home. But high tech demands a competent workforce — and that was when business discovered that something had gone badly wrong in U.S. high schools.

The examples are legion. New York Telephone, in an example that is frequently cited, had to screen fifty-seven thousand applicants to find twenty-one hundred who were qualified to perform entry-level technical jobs. The problem is obvious and so is its cause — according to a Department of Labor report on students' capabilities, "reading, writing, math and communication skills are largely inadequate for the demands of today's quality employers."

Even more disturbing to me are the comments made by the CEOs of two of Maine's largest corporations. Jim Orr of UNUM, a life and disability insurer in Portland, told me, "In reviewing job applicants, there is no comparison between American high-school graduates and their counterparts in Europe and Asia. The foreign applicants are far superior." Mickey Greene of Blue Cross and Blue Shield of Maine expresses the same idea just as forcefully: "Applicants coming to us right out of high school not only have unsatisfactory skills, but they seem to be getting worse every year."

The great problem, according to many employers, is that high schools in general have not kept pace with the needs of today's job market. As Dr. Daggett said in a speech in Maine in 1989, "Our schools are doing a wonderful job educating our kids for the jobs of the 1950s." Our vocational training is, in general, just as inadequate; it neither equals Japanese or European programs, nor prepares students for what they'll face when they leave school.

We have all heard the story of the U.S. company that must retrain new employees at a cost of eight hundred dollars per person, in contrast to the Japanese company that spends fifty-seven cents to do the same ("just hand the guy the manual"). Students with math achievement at about a fifth-grade level — and SAT scores show that they are a large majority — cannot enter the world of computerized factories and digitally controlled machines. And how can these students deal with the measurements required by the frequent tool changes in flexible manufacturing? Or learn statistical process control? Or tackle inventory management?

Without the ability to use and understand language beyond the fifth-grade level, how can the graduate read technical manuals, or handle a contract, or write a report?

If you look into the subject you would find that of twenty-four thousand U.S. high schools, seven thousand do not teach physics, four thousand do not teach chemistry, and two thousand teach no biology. Out of every one hundred high school students, twenty-five will drop out. Of the seventy-five who do graduate, twenty-five will have reading and math skills at a sixth-grade level. Less than one in four will make it through college. (This means, of course, that the vast majority of Americans rely on educational institutions other than four-year college to prepare them for entry into the workforce.)

For a decade now, experts have been telling us that the state of education in America is unacceptable. In fact, a nationwide report issued in 1982 by the National Commission on Excellence in Education declared America a "Nation at Risk." The commission pointed to lackluster educational initiatives and said that the nation was largely resting on its laurels.

The report was viewed as a clarion call to action. It demonstrated that while we had remained stagnant, education in other countries was improving dramatically. For the first time, America — for a century the world's leading industrialized nation — was falling behind.

The concept was alarming, but it did spur the nation to action. Countless reform efforts began, some in local schools, others statewide. The federal government began encouraging reform — and education became a popular and important issue across the country.

The report had another beneficial effect. Before 1982, governors were largely removed from education issues; most states had moved their chief education officials from under the governor's direct authority. The report served to encourage governors to reinvest themselves in education and make reform a top agenda item. Renewed interest by governors resulted in implementation of a flurry of changes. Initiatives encouraged schools to go "back to basics," and brought technology into the classroom. The most gifted students were given special encouragement through extra classes or summer schools, and universities were encouraged to develop "centers of excellence" that could transform education and training in America.

The 1980s also saw an explosion of partnerships between businesses and schools; a growth in developing new curriculum, assessment, and instructional materials; and the development of "reform networks" of schools. There were some notable achievements over the period, but by and large the activity was piecemeal, without widespread impact on the way students learn.

The implications of this piecemeal effort were alarming then and remain alarming today. America has more than one hundred thousand schools in more than sixteen thousand individual school systems. If reform is undertaken one school at a time, we will still be looking for solutions long after other nations have met their education needs. That's why it is important that reform address the *systemic* issues that lie at the underpinnings of education.

It is difficult to accept that we need to change a system that is so familiar, and has seemed successful. Making things even more challenging is the problem of envisioning what a new school system would look like.

To develop a vision for our schools — and some specific goals — in 1989 President Bush called a historic summit in Charlottesville, Virginia. I was one of the forty-nine governors who participated with the President in discussing the broad themes of education. The three-day summit, held just after the beginning of school in September, resulted in an unprecedented bipartisan consensus on national educational goals that we expect America to meet by the year 2000.

In issuing these goals, the President and the governors declared that "the time has come, for the first time in United States history, to establish clear national performance goals, goals that will make us internationally competitive."

We issued that statement because it had become abundantly clear that our education system needed to be changed; the goals serve as a vehicle to focus attention on where we stand, how far we have come, and how far we have to go to guarantee world-class education for all of our children.

By 1990, President Bush had established the National Education Goals Panel, which I now chair. Made up initially of governors and administration officials, the panel was carefully balanced between political parties and was charged with reporting progress and encouraging activities that could help achieve the goals.

For close to a year, the panel met in regional forums to develop the benchmarks of achievement. Until then, we were simply unable to assess our progress on educational improvement efforts because we had never gathered the necessary data.

The Goals Panel now issues an annual report and conducts important studies on technology in education, the effects of educational standards, and in a variety of other areas. Since its inception at the Education Summit in Charlottesville, the panel has become the nation's leading bipartisan organization advocating achievement of the goals, spurring an even greater effort among the states to reform our country's schools.

As of 1994, Congress and the Clinton administration have further expanded the efforts with passage of GOALS 2000: Educate America Act. This legislation sets the following National Education Goals to be met by the year 2000:

1. All children in America will start school ready to learn.
2. The high school graduation rate will increase to at least 90 percent.
3. All students will leave grades four, eight, and twelve having demonstrated competency in challenging subject matter including English, mathematics, science, foreign languages, civics and government, economics, arts, history, and geography, and every school in America will ensure that all students learn to use their minds well, so they may be prepared for responsible citizenship, further learning, and productive employment in our nation's modern economy.
4. U.S. students will be first in the world in mathematics and science achievement.
5. Every adult American will be literate and will possess

the knowledge and skills necessary to compete in a global economy and exercise the rights and responsibilities of citizenship.

6. Every school in the United States will be free of drugs, violence, and the unauthorized presence of firearms and alcohol and will offer a disciplined environment conducive to learning.

7. The nation's teaching force will have access to programs for the continued improvement of their professional skills and the opportunity to acquire the knowledge and skills needed to instruct and prepare all American students for the next century.

8. Every school will promote partnerships that will increase parental involvement and participation in promoting the social, emotional, and academic growth of children.

During my tenure in 1991–1992 as chairman of the Education Commission of the States (ECS), we focused on how to turn a school-by-school effort into a systemic restructuring — and found a remarkable consensus on key components of a successful strategy, including the need to: (a) create a vision; (b) develop and link policies; and (c) lay out strategies for implementation. We found there was particular agreement that all students can learn at significantly higher levels than currently taught. The efforts of ECS have been of great assistance to states, and significant restructuring efforts are being undertaken.

Some states, for example, are creating higher standards for students. Maine, Connecticut, and Vermont developed "common core" curricula that spelled out what students should know and be able to do. Teachers of science and mathematics developed twenty-first-century achievement standards that focus on problem solving and inquiry rather than rote memorization. And a variety of states — from California to Maine — have begun developing "frameworks" that establish benchmarks to measure achievement statewide.

Through improved assessment methods, states are also holding schools accountable for learning — a dramatic change from the past, when attendance was demanded, but not necessarily achievement. Vermont and California now use portfolios that demonstrate student ability; in Maine, we have revamped our fourth grade, eighth grade, and eleventh grade assessment tests to examine performance-based thinking. A written essay in the Maine Education Assessment, for example, evaluates students' thought processes — rather than simply their ability to mark right or wrong on a multiple-choice test.

States have also looked to decentralization, encouraging bureaucratic change by easing regulations. Some, like Kentucky, have encouraged site-based decision making that gives an increased stake to teachers and local administrators. Others, like South Carolina, have adopted "total quality management," applying the organizational theories of W. Edwards Deming to school processes. And significantly, many states have begun reducing the burden of state regulation, eliminating micromanagement by state agencies. In Maine, for example, my commissioner of education offered to waive every state regulation for schools and districts willing to commit to student outcomes (and, of course, student safety).

States have placed more emphasis on teacher and staff development, and encouraged schools to provide the time for teachers to talk to one another — answering a consistent complaint within the existing system. From improved student-teaching, to encouraging communication between colleges and local schools, states have made numerous attempts to improve education. The Southern Maine Partnership, for instance, brought together university faculty and local school staff, with the result that teacher preparation was significantly upgraded.

Yet even with all of the diverse attempts over the past decade, no state has successfully pulled together reform efforts. As the National Education Goals Report of 1992 said: "Many students continue to leave American schools without ever being seriously challenged, without ever fully knowing what they are capable of learning and doing, and without having gained the tools and skills they need to survive and prosper."

As the current chairman of the National Education Goals Panel, I have seen how much more we need to do. Our progress has been wholly insufficient to meet our goals for the year 2000. We lag in achieving every major goal, and we do not meet world-class standards.

Our most recent report issued a wake-up call to the American people. We found:

1. Almost half of American youth start life behind, and never receive the support they need to catch up. The

panel found that 45 percent of American children are born into circumstances that predict a high risk of school failure; these are often health factors such as the mother smoking during pregnancy. Alarmingly, only 53 percent of preschoolers are read to every day by their parents.

2. In grades K-12, most American children cannot perform at the levels necessary for success in today's world. The 1992 report found that fewer than 1 in 5 fourth graders, 1 in 5 twelfth graders, and 1 in 4 eighth graders understood complex mathematical problems. All too often, our students lag not because they cannot understand the problems — but because schools simply do not teach to a challenging level.

3. Despite progress made over the past decade, about 12 percent of American adolescents fail to complete high school. These citizens face a grim future: dropouts in the 1990s will earn less than half as much as someone who dropped out in 1973. They are simply not qualified for anything but the most menial jobs.

4. Today's schools are full of barriers, even for those who want to work hard. More than half our students do not feel completely safe — and complain that misbehavior by others hinders their learning. Almost two of every ten students have been offered drugs while in school; one in ten has brought a weapon to school *in the last month!*

5. In a country in which a highly skilled workforce is critical, many Americans have only mediocre basic literacy. And even these average skills are declining. All but a small percentage of Americans can read and write, but American literacy is based on old

standards. Today, mechanics need to work with computers, to understand statistical quality control, and to read complex manuals. Simply put, the American people don't understand how drastically the world — and the workplace — has changed. Fifty-seven percent of American workers believe that their skills will be adequate in the years ahead, compared to just 13 percent of Japanese workers.

The evidence is clear. Our schools are not making the grade. Our students are in jeopardy of being schooled to fail.

And the level of failure is even worse in inner city schools, where funding and societal problems contribute to an education system in crisis. Jonathan Kozol writes of the Chicago schools in his book *Savage Inequalities:*

> Some 6,700 students enter ninth grade in these 18 schools each year. Only 300 of these students . . . both graduate and read at or above the national average. Those very few who graduate and go to college rarely read well enough to handle college-level courses. At the city's community colleges, which receive most of their students from Chicago's public schools, the noncompletion rate is 97 percent. . . .
>
> Looking at these failure rates again — and particularly at the reading scores of high-school graduates — it is difficult to know what argument a counselor can make to tell a failing student that she ought to stay in school, except

perhaps to note that a credential will, statistically, improve her likelihood of finding work. . . . For many, many students at Chicago's non-selective high schools, it is hard to know if a decision to drop out of school, no matter how much we discourage it, is not, in fact, a logical decision.

How did this happen? Why have students not bound for college been shunted aside? The answer lies in our national history.

For its first two hundred years, the United States stayed ahead of the competition and prospered, and almost everyone's standard of living went up. During those two centuries — until about 1980 — there was no societal imperative to educate everyone up to the college, or even the high-school, level. That meant that the best education was largely lavished on approximately the top third of students, those who were considered college material.

In their recent book, *The Learning Gap,* authors Harold Stevenson and James Stigler cite one of the most difficult aspects of achieving education reform in America. Their conclusion is that Americans are not yet committed to change. Although a study issued by the Education Excellence Partnership and done by Chilton Research Service in September 1993 shows that a majority of Americans now disagree that "some schools need improvement, but not mine," this is the first such finding in a significant national survey. While a majority of Americans support education reform in theory, most surveys have found that they have not carried that support to their local schools. Stevenson and Stigler explain the phenomenon this way:

> Americans are satisfied with their children's education partly because they have lacked a meaningful gauge by which to evaluate how well their children are doing. Because most children pass from one grade to the next, and parents see happy faces rather than grades on many of their children's assignments, they assume that their children are doing a good job. This is clearly not true.

The Education Commission of the States conducted a survey in 1993 of educators, students, and businesses to find out how each group felt schools were doing in educating their students. The results are revealing.

Seventy-five percent of the teachers and administrators felt the schools were doing a good job in meeting their goals. Seventy percent of the students felt the schools were doing a good job. But only 25 percent of the businesses surveyed thought the schools were doing an adequate job.

The more I have thought about how the numbers could be so different, the more it occurred to me that they reflect expectations. For at least fifty years, the challenge to our schools has been to send more students to college. And if that is the goal, the educators are correct in thinking our schools are succeeding. More of our students are receiving a postsecondary education than ever before. Likewise, since most students are being asked to do more than they want to do in school, it is not surprising they would think the school is doing a good job! Few students have any point of reference other than their own school, so it is difficult for them to compare.

Businesses, however, are in a different position. They see students coming both from high schools and from colleges. I believe the reason businesses have such a low estimation of our schools is that when they think of high schools, they think only of the students who are coming directly from the school to work. They forget that the students who are coming to them from college also went to the same high schools and, after completing their postsecondary studies, are generally adequate employees. The ECS survey reveals that students coming directly out of our high schools are not adequate employees, and that is because we have designed an educational system that is not providing them with the tools they need to succeed in the world of work.

Because of educators' push to send more students to college, I worry that U.S. students' poor international test scores will simply lead to an increase in spending on the top third of our students, and, once again, the rest of our children will be neglected. It is these neglected students whom we must equip to understand and run today's electronic technology. And we must equip them in high school. We ignore them at our peril. Our schools must be revamped so that those who aren't among the best students will be given an education that makes them ready to meet the technology of the twenty-first century head on.

Indeed, many of the nation's finest school reform efforts are centered around the philosophy that all young people can learn — a radical departure from the old beliefs that some kids are born dumb and will always be behind.

I got to know an outstanding reformer, Dr. Theodore R. Sizer, during my year as chairman of the ECS. Ted Sizer has devoted the last ten years to improving the quality of U.S. schools and founded the Coalition of Essential Schools in 1984 to improve education, especially at the secondary-school level. Sizer's essential schools are built around nine principles aimed at helping students use their minds well. The schools, which focus on student needs rather than simply curriculum or teaching methods, encourage students to question and reason while in school and, through personalized instruction, give students enhanced responsibility for their own learning.

"The only way [the new curriculum] can work is if teachers can work with kids when they make a mistake, so the kids can learn from their mistakes, and that means a whole lot fewer kids," Sizer said. "If you get kids into the habit of teaching themselves, you can cover much more. If you make libraries and all kinds of other tools accessible to kids, then they can all learn on their own. But you have to start young, even at elementary school."

With their unique orientation toward student learning, Sizer's essential schools involve all students in their education and have shown promising results. Unfortunately, most schools have not yet adopted the common principles; many still guide the top students toward higher education, allowing others to languish in general education.

Ensuring that all students do learn means taking into consideration the varying needs of all students, and we must especially consider the needs of many students in minority populations. Our schools, to a great degree, have again become separate but unequal. The student body of big city schools is predominantly low-income black or Hispanic. Suburban schools are mostly middle to upper income; economic standing, not race, is the key factor here. In any case, from 1970 to 1993, the number of white students enrolled in Detroit public schools went from 98,000 to 14,000; in Atlanta, from 50,000 to 4,000; in Los Angeles, from 324,000 to 85,000. As Mary Jordan recently reported in the *Washington Post:* "Increasingly there are two tiers of schools in major American cities: free schools for the low-income, and schools costing $1,000 to $10,000 for everyone else."

Jonathan Kozol recalls his impression of inner city schools:

> The schools were surrounded frequently by signs that indicated DRUG-FREE ZONE. Their doors were guarded. Police sometimes patrolled the halls. The windows of the schools were often covered with steel grates. Taxi drivers flatly refused to take me to some of these schools and would deposit me a dozen blocks away, in border areas beyond which they refused to go. . . . I was dismayed to walk or ride for blocks and blocks through neighborhoods where every face

was black, where there were simply *no white people anywhere.*

Minorities, too, have sorted themselves out by income; wealthier minority families have moved to the suburbs. The students from better-off families attend schools like the Milton Academy in suburban Boston, just like upper-middle-class white children. But there are precious few of these families; most have been left behind. Unemployment rates for young blacks and Latinos in the largest U.S. cities are officially estimated to run between 25 and 40 percent but, as Jack Wuest, executive director of the Alternative Schools Network, notes: "Over 75 to 80 percent of minority youth are not ever counted in the official unemployment rate because they aren't even looking for work. They often live in neighborhoods where there are no jobs to be found."

A number of organizations have been trying to address the problems of at-risk kids. Jobs for America's Graduates, Inc. (JAG), is one that works. One hundred twenty-five thousand at-risk and disadvantaged young people have been through the program over the past decade in five hundred high schools in twenty-two states. These are young people that the schools have told the local JAG staff are "least likely" to either complete school or get a job upon leaving school. Typically, the students are low achievers; over one third were suspended or expelled from school, over 60 percent are poor as defined by federal poverty guidelines, and nearly half live with single parents.

By applying the concentrated attention of a dedicated staff member (known as a job specialist) who is held personally accountable for the success of thirty-five to forty students, combined with a motivational student organization that spotlights student successes, employment opportunities provided by the business community, and a direct linkage from school to support in the workplace for nine months, the program delivers results.

Ninety percent of the young people achieve either a high-school diploma or a GED within nine months of what would have been their regular high-school graduation date. Ninety percent! That proves we can, in fact, not only meet but exceed Goal 2 of the National Education Goals, that of a 90 percent graduation rate — and we can achieve it today if we set our minds to it.

Furthermore, 80 percent of the young people, at the end of the nine months of support in the workplace, are either on the job, in the military, or enrolled in postsecondary training. That is nearly double the rate of similar young people without the benefit of the program. Remarkably, all of this can be done at the cost of about one thousand dollars per student for the eighteen months of service — well under half the national average for similar programs, most of which do not have the nine-month follow-up.

Some other national programs have also stood the test of time. WAVE, Inc. (Work, Achievement, Values, and Education), is such an organization. Established in 1969 as 70,001, Inc., it changed its name to WAVE in 1990. WAVE programs build self-esteem and the motivation needed to succeed, while providing the structure that young people in at-risk communities need. WAVE has demonstrated what can be done to help high-school dropouts gain a high-school diploma and move successfully into employment. Today, they are engaged in a major effort, in hundreds of schools across the country, to sharply reduce the dropout rate through a new approach in curriculum and teacher orientation.

Cities in Schools is one of the oldest success stories. Established in the 1960s, it reaches fifty-six thousand young people today in 131 communities. Its key objective is to bring the cities into the school. This strategy engages young people directly in what is going on in their communities — especially the business community — while they are still in school. It is particularly aimed at bringing community services and resources to bear on young people in need — and it clearly produces results in improving the retention rate, the attitudes of young people, and their expectations about the world upon leaving school.

American Express reports that its National Academy Foundation, led by former senator and labor secretary Bill Brock and presidential counselor Vernon Jordan, has had solid success in its first four years of existence, establishing "schools within schools" focused on distinct occupational areas. Tourism, public sector management, finance — all are "academies" within schools that promise specialized skill and career training, integrated with the other academic subjects, to develop skills required for specific jobs in the future.

All of these programs have had success, but the impact has been at the margins.

They demonstrate that there is hope even in the

inner cities. The real question, then, is why are our schools producing so many students who have neither the skills required for employment nor the ability to master new work skills quickly?

Changing the Old Model

James Kadamus, former assistant commissioner in New York's Office of Higher and Continuing Education, answers that question by saying, "Work is moving to a new training paradigm, while schools tend to stick with the old model."

In his book *The Children's Machine,* Seymour Papert examines ways that visionary teachers have used computers to dramatically improve teaching. Papert imagines two groups of time travelers from an earlier century — a group of surgeons and a group of schoolteachers. Through this parable, Papert examines the reaction of the surgeons, bewildered by modern medical equipment — "the rituals of antiseptics and anesthesia, the beeping electronics, and even the bright lights, all so familiar to television audiences, would be utterly unfamiliar to them" — contrasting that with the response of the schoolteachers, who would feel at home in today's classrooms, where very little has changed.

> In the wake of the startling growth of science and technology in our recent past, some areas of human activity have undergone megachange — telecommunications, entertainment, transportation and medicine among them. . . . Why, through a period when so much human activity has been revolutionized, have we not seen a

comparable change in the way we help our children learn?

The old model is a classroom with a teacher at a desk in front, who lectures and draws diagrams on the blackboard. Students listen, take notes, answer questions, and recite. Their relationship resembles traditional communication between manager and employee. Eve Bither, my former commissioner of education who now works for the U.S. Department of Education, has summed up the situation very graphically. The schoolroom, she says, is "the only place left in America where the relatively young sit and watch the relatively old work."

But, as we have seen, modern production is now a series of complex problems solved through teamwork. Management works differently, providing guidance rather than governance; management has become a resource, not a ruler.

This altered structure makes radically new demands on employees. The student who now moves easily from school to industry is self-reliant; possesses the conceptual skills to analyze problems, decide on tactics, and provide solutions; and is endowed with the communication skills needed to be part of a team.

This student will also be capable of the lifetime learning necessary to keep up with the astonishing pace of change in the high-tech, information, and service economy of tomorrow. Soon people will not only change jobs several times in their working years, but change entire careers as well. Students must possess specific abilities and broader capabilities. Skills can become outmoded, but the ability to learn never does.

As an example of the new interaction between learning and work, Kadamus cites Courseware, the software program IBM uses in a worldwide instructional system for its employees. "On any given day," he says, "IBM has twenty-two thousand employees engaged in classroom training . . . a true merging of work and learning."

UNUM matches IBM's commitment to training and support as part of its revamped decision-making and management structure. Each of the company's four thousand employees receives between one and two weeks of training each year to improve technical and team skills. The training is integral to UNUM's corporate mission, and to further encourage team building, UNUM now determines total pay based upon department or team results, not individual performance alone.

None of this is news to the best secondary-school teachers, or to the best vocational training instructors. I don't believe that the failure of students to achieve higher standards lies with their teachers, but within our educational system. Until we reform that system, despite heroic efforts on the part of teachers, many of our children will fail. Lamar Alexander, a former secretary of education, once likened the present educational system to the old pony express. Even the best riders and the fastest horses were no match for the new technology of that time, the telegraph.

In the majority of our high schools, in spite of changes in the workplace, learning remains a discipline unconnected to the outside world, the world of work. These schools evaluate students by textbook criteria. Students are not given the skills they will need in the real world.

In *The Double Helix of Education and the Economy,* Sue Berryman and Thomas Bailey say that, kindergarten through high school, education is badly out of sync with changes taking place in the new business and industrial environment. They point out that schools "routinely violate what we know about how people learn most effectively and the conditions under which they apply their knowledge to new situations." They argue that schools separate learning from the real-life situations that make learning meaningful: "Human beings . . . learn best when they are fully and actively engaged in solving problems that mean something to them." They further point out that cognitive scientists know that children learn naturally through an informal kind of "apprenticeship" — which is exactly the mode of learning that is used in the reengineered and revitalized workplace.

It is the teachers who, before all else, must be re-educated. They must learn to perform their role differently. First, they must avoid what Berryman, former director of the Institute on Education and the Economy at Columbia Teachers College, calls the six common mistakes in present-day education. To do that they must realize:

1. Skills are not like building blocks; individuals do not have to learn the basics before they learn specific technical or problem-solving skills.

2. The learner is not a blank slate, as is commonly supposed. The traditional curriculum ignores what is already in the student's head.
3. Education often has an inappropriate image of the learner as a passive receptacle — and of learning as the process of simply pouring knowledge into the brain of the learner.
4. Skills are often taught in isolation from practical experience with the result that surprisingly few theoretical principles are transferred to practice.
5. Separating learning-to-know and learning-to-do is dysfunctional.
6. Knowledge and skills are often taught in settings that do not simulate those in which the work must be performed — i.e., the teaching occurs out of context.

I believe that today's schools are the institutions primarily responsible for the economic future of their students. All other virtues of education are important but secondary as we approach the millennium. Nevertheless, our system has always tended to insist on a false division between academic study and vocational learning, losing sight of the fact that mathematics was born out of trade, geometry out of land surveying, and prose out of the need to communicate information. Berryman and Bailey advocate a kind of reinvention of teaching, organizing it on the principles of cognitive apprenticeship, and allowing students to learn through observation and experience.

Today, few high schools are aware of being "primarily responsible for the economic future of their students." A 1991 National Association of Manufacturers and Towers Perrin survey found that 40 percent of NAM members surveyed had trouble modernizing their technology; 33 percent were "having serious difficulties reorganizing work activities because many employees cannot learn new tasks"; and 25 percent were "having problems teaching employees statistical process control or other quality-enhancing techniques." The obvious conclusion is that government, education, and business must understand and agree about this huge national problem and work out a tripartite solution.

It used to be that the educated and the uneducated held each other in disdain; war movies show enlisted men who scoff at the officers as college wimps, and officers who treat enlisted men as children. But those attitudes are as outdated as the classroom with the podium in front. The new world of work has blurred the old distinctions between school and job, manager and worker. The technological knowledge required for nearly every decent job today has effectively breached the barrier between the educated and the uneducated. Now everyone must be educated; it is only a matter of type and degree.

There is an urgent need for a profound overhaul of our educational methods and goals. Tinkering around the edges of our present system won't produce the change we must have. No longer is it enough to offer only one third of our students a first-rate education. The requirements for success in today's and tomorrow's job market demand new skills and knowledge from every single one of our young.

While I was chairman of the ECS in 1991, I led the organization's debate on systemic change in education, built on a belief that piecemeal change would never have a widespread impact on improving schools and reaching the national goals. We knew that the system needed to change. Our experience in education shows that the overall education system discourages innovation, prevents success from spreading, and slows change to a crawl.

To improve the system, we set forth an education agenda for change that built in principles of employee empowerment and teamwork that W. Edwards Deming made popular in his organizational theories on total quality management. First, we urged states to begin with a "vision" showing what kids should know and be able to do. The vision would guide school policies and decisions that could be linked to support that vision, and later to lay out the plans for implementation. We also laid out the case for improving teacher training and helping teachers understand why change is important — and that it can, at times, be a daunting task.

Apart from fundamental misconceptions and outdated attitudes, one of the main obstacles to redesigning our schools is the bureaucracy of our educational establishment, which has become many-layered and deeply entrenched. Authority is vested in a bewildering array of bodies ranging from federal to regional, state, district, local — right down to the school itself. There are, for instance, eighty different vocational-technical programs in California schools, according to Gerald Hayward, deputy director of the National Center for Research in Vocational Training. Their very extensive distribution and lack of coordination makes the system insufficiently responsive to desperately needed change.

The diverse nature of many school programs is not the only problem, however. I remember, as chairman of the ECS, talking with groups of parents and students who seemed unconvinced that schools need to change — at all. Too many people, satisfied with their own education, don't see why change makes a difference. And the schools don't help either: though individual teachers may be outstanding in their areas, our education system tends to reward those who don't make waves instead of those who are constantly seeking better ways of doing things.

And overall, too few people understand how to lead reform efforts: our education system swallows innovation in a vast sea of programs and old ideas.

The problem is all too clear. The world has changed. The way goods and services are produced has undergone an even greater revolution. Highly skilled, computer-literate teams are the wave of the future. Our schools are not developing players for those teams, and we are not encouraging or rewarding them to do so.

That has to change. The choice is stark: either solve this problem or lose our lead in the great contest of nations.

4

The Consequences
of Inaction

IT IS A GREAT TEMPTATION for those who are doing well to believe that everything will stay the same. It won't. In our time the pace of change has accelerated to unprecedented speed, and the world of work and the world economic order are both profoundly and irrevocably altered because of it.

To ignore the challenge of change is to succumb to shortsighted complacency, to the fantasy that the world will remain forever as it is.

Global competition has hurled a challenge at U.S. business, which was once unrivaled in the world. But that is no longer true. We may still be number one in productivity, but our lead has shrunk. Many U.S. companies have responded vigorously to the new economic realities and have accepted the need for change. Some have downsized, using electronic technology and robots to grow leaner and meaner. Others have shipped jobs to places where labor costs are lower. Some companies have combined the two strategies. As a result, productivity and growth have increased. But these changes have brought not more jobs, but fewer.

The Best of Times?

The famous Charles Dickens quotation, "It was the best of times, it was the worst of times," can probably describe any period in history, but it is especially applicable to the United States today. We see peerless productivity and a stagnant or falling standard of living; the best and the worst commingling. At first glance, this contradiction seems an affront to common sense: how can we be working better and living worse?

The paradox of a rising level of productivity and a falling standard of living is one of the many reasons that the U.S. business scene is such a bewildering place, just as puzzling for the "suit-and-tie employed" as for the new graduate just entering the job market. The situation is cloudy and is likely to remain so for quite some time (to be expected in a great age of transition).

Not only are there fewer new jobs, but many of our young people find, on entering the job market, that they face a demand for skills they don't have. Even those who have jobs live in dread of seeing them fall victim to the changes in the way U.S. business is conducted.

It isn't just the old-fashioned assembly line worker whose job has vanished. As business reengineers, middle management often finds itself obsolete. In fact, the unemployment rate for white-collar workers and blue-collar workers now runs neck and neck.

I found a good example of this across-the-board

downsizing at Osram Sylvania in Waldoboro, Maine. In 1987, its Sylvania Coil Operations plant employed 278 people — 176 blue-collar and 102 white-collar — and turned out 4.75 million coils a day. By 1993, the plant employed 202 people — 130 blue-collar and 72 white-collar — and produced 5.15 million coils a day.

The fact that white-collar employees are no longer immune to productivity-enhancing measures has meant that throughout 1991 and 1992, a number of white-collar unemployed support groups grew up in our major employment areas. I remember talking to one member of a group, a forty-one-year-old man who had worked for a high-tech company as an engineer for eight years. He used his intelligence, know-how, and graduate degree in engineering to rise to the position of quality control engineer — when all of a sudden he was terminated. His duties were integrated into other positions as the company enhanced technology and cut expenses to survive the downturn of the 1990s. His fears were crystallized when his employer told him that even when the economy improved, the company wouldn't be expanding white-collar positions, because they'd learned how to streamline operations and reduce costs.

At the time that a company replaces the assembly line with robots (in 1982 there were thirty-two thousand robots in the United States; by 1989 the number had grown to 1.3 million; the projection for 1995 is 20 to 24 million), it usually introduces other technological changes as well.

QR Industries, according to Willard A. Daggett in the November/December 1990 issue of *North Carolina*

Education, serves as a classic example. It manufactures steel products including clamps that secure hoses in General Motors cars. In 1985 the company had three hundred people making clamps. Then it brought in robots, computers, and bar codes. This technology not only speeded up production; it also increased precision. Today, QR Industries has seventeen people making clamps.

It wasn't just assembly line workers at QR who lost their jobs. There were people in accounts receivable who were made obsolete by direct-to-computer accounting, as were their opposite numbers at GM in the accounts payable department. True, the changes that modernized the company made it more profitable. They also put 283 people out of work.

Timberland also made radical changes in its business procedures. Recognizing that a major shift in its market — from large department stores to small boutiques — called for frequent small deliveries rather than occasional large ones, the company installed sophisticated electronic technology to keep track of inventory and multiple small orders. At the same time, they merged the credit-verification and order departments. The company's executives saw the electronic highway as a two-way street. Customers can now send in their orders to a computer. From there, the orders are routed rapidly and directly via network to the manufacturing division.

The revolution that has helped Osram Sylvania, QR Industries, Timberland, and other companies illustrates perfectly the way in which U.S. business has to update itself in order to survive and compete in the new economic world order, and the potentially devastating impact of those changes on employees.

No change, economic or social, can occur without human cost. In our country today that situation can be summed up by three small words: fewer new jobs. Not only has job growth slowed, but the very nature of work itself has changed radically. In the future, employment will grow in "smart jobs." The reengineering revolution means that practically all work — not just technical, white-collar, or managerial — is being transformed into smart jobs. Reengineering has created new team systems, which carry through entire manufacturing or service processes. These systems demand workers with a good basic education, technical skills, and a capacity to make decisions. Companies will be looking for fewer and fewer old-style production workers, and for more and more team workers. For anyone entering the job market, that translates into a demand for educated employees.

One example of "smart jobs" can be found at the Winthrop, Maine, warehouse of wholesale and retail food distributor Hannaford Brothers Company. A design team, made up of a cross section of mostly hourly workers, was formed at the warehouse to develop a new work environment — new ways of doing work in a new culture. Teams of workers are now doing many tasks formerly done by supervisors or specialists, such as hiring, firing, discipline, and performance reviews. They are also making key daily operating decisions like work assignments, scheduling, use of overtime, inventory adjustments, and training assignments. The workers are now both working and supervising. The former supervisors are doing more coaching, teaching, and mentoring. As Hugh Farrington, president and chief executive officer of Hannaford Brothers, succinctly put it, "After the new design was implemented, productivity, including all development and training time, has improved. Total operating costs have been reduced because workers are working not harder, but smarter."

Quality can be even more important in some high-tech businesses. Steve Graebert, manager of a General Electric plant in Bangor, Maine, told me about his struggle to increase productivity and quality. GE Bangor is a division of GE's Naval and Drive Turbine Systems Department, and produces steam turbines. Steam turbines have a lifetime of between thirty and sixty years, and downtime due to malfunction can cost the owner $10,000 per hour. Although this makes reliability and repairability a competitive issue, the long lifetime of the turbines also limits change.

In Bangor, however, global competition has brought change. Today, the plant must improve three to five times faster than just ten years ago — simply to stay competitive. "Five years ago, we could be proud of a 3 percent per year productivity rate. Today, a rate of 10 percent per year is required," Graebert told me.

To meet this challenge, GE Bangor has chosen to engage employees in the process by informing them of business goals, encouraging their involvement, and giving them the education and technical and problem-solving skills they need to meet advanced challenges.

In late 1989, GE Bangor began an aggressive training program to teach all of its 450 employees state-of-the-art metal removal technology. The program was coupled with an increased push in total quality management and "just-in-time" techniques. Every employee was also given forty hours of training in analytical problem-solving and team-building skills. The company also initiated work teams built around product lines to encourage entrepreneurship and empower employees.

GE's results in Bangor have been outstanding. The manufacturing cycle time has dropped from ten weeks to fewer than ten days, increasing productivity 40 percent. Sales have continued to grow steadily, despite a 50 percent reduction in defense-related orders. Although GE quality has been certified by both the U.S. military and the International Standards Organization, quality costs have decreased more than 50 percent, while time lost due to accidents runs only one third the industry average.

"We've been able to accomplish these improvements with such speed because our machine tool operators are not just operating the machines," Graebert says. "They're also writing quality plans, running problem-solving sessions, buying machine tools, developing cutting tools directly with suppliers, evaluating and approving suggestions of their peers, designing fixtures, and bidding on jobs. In other words, they participate on an equal footing and have even replaced traditional 'management' personnel in virtually every aspect of running a globally competitive business."

Given these kinds of changes in the workplace, our failure to change the way we prepare students for the world of work will mean an even greater division between what some social commentators call the "haves" and the "have-nots" in our society. The new have-nots will be those without training and without the ability to acquire the new skills demanded in today's workplace.

Now, more than ever, education is a significant determinant of a person's economic future. U.S. Department of Labor data show that in the 1990s, both men and women need post high-school education to stay above the median income level. It is also clear from the data that workers with the least education are the ones whose standard of living is dropping the fastest. If current trends continue, the disparity can only increase. Those whose few dollars buy less and less will find their small stake in the United States further diminished. The old saying that "the rich get richer and the poor get poorer" may, unfortunately, be only too true if changes are not made. Those with the luck to inherit wealth or the skills to acquire it will be increasingly separated from the rest of society, which will be made up of a shrinking and besieged middle class, the working poor, and lastly, the underclass. If this happens, we will acquire one of the main structural characteristics of a third world society.

It may seem preposterous and alarmist even to consider using the term "third world" to describe the United States. It has associations — poverty and shoddy goods made by cheap labor — that don't seem to apply to our country. But the term refers to the structure of a society and its place vis-à-vis developed and productive nations. The specter of becoming a third world nation has become a pressing concern for many serious and significant thinkers.

A Third World United States?

Edward Luttwak, currently director of Geo-Economics at the Center for Strategic and International Studies in Washington, D.C., and former consultant to the National Security Council, the White House chief of staff, the State Department, and the Department of Defense, is hardly someone on the intellectual fringe. Yet his recent book, *The Endangered American Dream,* raises this very issue in its subtitle: *How to Stop the United States from Becoming a Third World Country and How to Win the Geo-Economic Struggle for Industrial Supremacy.*

In the very first paragraph, the book describes a U.S. traveler returning home from Europe and Asia to find a country less orderly and efficient than those he has visited. There is a threadbare feel about the United States these days.

One of Luttwak's chapters is entitled, "When Will We Become a Third World Country?" His answer is: around the year 2020, if we do nothing to alter current trends. This is a most conservative view. According to Luttwak, simply by continuing today's trends, in 2020 the average European will be twice as productive as the average American, whereas the average Japanese will be five times more productive. The U.S. elite will continue to live well, but everyone else will fare poorly indeed.

The cities and their infrastructures will continue to deteriorate. The strain on social services will rise, making less money available for universities, libraries, and museums; and life is always dimmer without the stimulation of the arts.

It is not a pretty picture.

Trust in a democracy depends on economic justice. People play by the rules as long as they seem fair. It is unlikely that trust in the American way of life could survive a steep decline in the standard of living among a large part of the population. The response could very likely be social turmoil, bringing with it a further erosion of trust and stability: a perfect breeding ground for crime, drugs, and social unrest.

In some parts of America that is already here. "On average, someone is hit by gunfire in New York City every 88 minutes." This chilling statistic appeared in a November 15, 1993, article in the *New York Times,* entitled "Trying to Stanch Blood in an Urban War Zone." The article continues:

> More people were murdered in New York than died of colon cancer or breast cancer or from all accidents combined. More than twice as many were murdered as were killed in motor vehicle accidents. Homicide is the leading cause of death among men and women between the ages of 15 and 24. Among men between 25 and 34, homicide is the second leading cause of death after AIDS. Until New Yorkers turn 55, homicide is among the 10 highest causes of death in every age group, including among infants under 1 year old.

The article also focused on the petition by Alliant Techsystems for a Department of Defense grant to "transform sonar technology developed for detecting submarines into devices that would alert urban police forces to gunfire." Capable of split-second analysis of sound, the detection devices could be mounted on utility poles.

It was impossible to read this article without feeling a keenly painful sense of irony. The technology that helped us win the cold war may be used to help us fight the war in our own streets; a war that, so far, we seem incapable of winning.

Some might argue that New York is an exception and that its problems don't really apply to the rest of the country. There is a touch of truth in that — about one out of every ten murders in the United States is committed in New York City — but only a touch. The spread of crime in our country is hardly confined to New York — after all, our nation's capital is the murder capital of the country, a dubious honor it snatched from Detroit. Crime, as well as the fear of crime, has insinuated itself into every corner of American life. And street crime has the same kind of spreading, poisonous ripple effect as terrorism — a crime may directly harm only one person, but the reporting of it in the news strikes fear into the hearts of millions. Violence grows worse, and fear grows with it. It is precisely that fear which corrodes the quality of daily life.

It's no secret whose finger is on most of the triggers being squeezed every eighty-eight minutes in New York City. It belongs to the young people who see only one way to acquire wealth, position, and power: through the sale of narcotics and its attendant violence. They find a ready market for their drugs among their peers as well as in society as a whole.

The scale of this problem is overwhelming. In

1987, 4 percent of the population of Washington, D.C. — some twenty-four thousand people — were thought to be dealing drugs. Those drug dealers had a net income of $300 million. Before taxes — and after. As Luttwak remarks acerbically, "For the adolescent black male dropouts of Washington, D.C., who have very few job opportunities and those mostly at minimum wage (or less), drug dealing is the only career option of significance, and those who enter the trade are making a rational choice based on correct information."

Yet poverty is not the sole source of crime. Otherwise the rich would all be innocent! Helmsleys and Boeskys, Keatings and Milkins, are as much a part of the story of our times as young people slaughtering each other with sophisticated weapons. Yes, crime may be rooted in our nature; the first event in the Bible after the expulsion from Eden is a crime. Cain slew Abel. But it is also plain that people with a stake in society have a stake in society's rules. And those who feel that they have no chance at the freedoms and pleasures of security and stability will be drawn to drugs, some for the solace they provide, others for the income.

In a December 1993 op-ed piece in the *New York Times* entitled "America's Job Disaster," Bob Herbert draws the inescapable conclusion: "There is a violent crime emergency in the United States, and there is an employment crisis. The policymakers seem unable to understand the ways in which they are linked, and the degree to which the former is driven by the latter."

Of course, crime is no stranger to U.S. cities, and we should retain a historical perspective — Chicago in the 1920s was a violent place. Yet, in those days of battling gangs, there was a certain professional etiquette observed — gangsters killed each other; innocent by-standers were rarely struck by gunfire. That would have been considered unprofessional, a disgrace. No babies died in the St. Valentine's Day massacre.

Even crime has changed. Now it is the ran-domness, the very lack of limits, that makes the new class of criminals so dangerous. The real measure of the quality of life in any society is found not only in hous-ing, health services, and the like, but in the value people place on themselves. In a successful society a majority of the people lead lives that they feel are worthwhile. The fear that your life could suddenly be snuffed by a stray bullet makes everything else meaningless. A "senseless killing" is an expression we have heard many times on the news — but a senseless death can make life seem senseless as well.

The United States has always offered its people hope and the chance to rise from the bottom. Sociolo-gists call it upward mobility. Others call it the Ameri-can dream. Throughout its history, this country has always been reinfused with the fresh energy and ambi-tion of new immigrants who were ready to work in the hope of a better life. They kept the economy vigorous and innovative. And society was kept stable through promises fulfilled and a social contract honored. Seen in another way, the hope of success becomes a way for society to blow off some of the steam that accumulates whenever there is a great gap between rich and poor. In the United States of the future, the United States that will result if the need for change is ignored, that valve will be clogged shut. And sooner or later a clogged valve erupts.

Nearly all well-paying work requires a new kind of education. Even among those who have this advantage, the competition is fierce. In the future much will be demanded before success can be achieved. If we are not careful, society may well become divided into those who have mastered the complicated rules of the new competition and those who'll never even have the chance to learn the rules.

At the present time, social resentment is mostly confined to crime. But that could change. Terrorism, which is politics expressed as crime, could haunt our cities as it does in other countries. If the road upward is in fact closed, people at the bottom can justly complain that they have no other route to take. It would then be only a matter of time before that resentment began to organize itself into a quest for power more threatening than a stickup or a drug deal.

This is, of course, a vision of the United States in deterioration. What makes it most troubling is that it doesn't seem so far-fetched.

Of course, the country has survived worse times — the Great Depression, for example. But this current crisis gnaws insidiously at the foundations of our society. The Great Depression was nothing if not dramatic. When people are lined up for soup or selling apples in the street, it's hard to deny you've got trouble on your hands. Today, the disparities are far less visible, and those of us living in relative comfort often choose to ignore them.

It's not that we don't know about today's problems. Nowadays we have more information than people ever dreamed of back in the 1930s. But what are we doing with this information? Some people prefer awareness rather than action, fooling themselves into thinking that being well informed is enough. Others become numbed by bad news. Yet others distance themselves from the unending reports of plant closings and youth violence, believing "it can't possibly happen here."

In matters of survival, there are no excuses. There is only action or inaction. The court of history will laugh at our complaint that we failed to take up the challenge of a changing world because we were too flooded with information. Instead, that court will reply that the information was readily available and only the effort to understand and act on it intelligently was required. Having failed to do so, we would rightly be found guilty of gross negligence — and for those of us in public office, dereliction of duty.

Maine is the northeasternmost point in the continental United States, and maybe that makes it a good vantage point for looking out on the United States and the rest of the world. When I looked at Maine, I saw jobs disappearing and food vanishing from the dinner table. As governor, I could not help but be deeply concerned. Where, I asked myself, were the jobs going, and why?

I saw that some of the jobs were leaving for countries where the labor was either cheaper or more highly skilled. And the rest of the jobs were just plain disappearing, no longer relevant in the new world of work.

Then, as I have mentioned earlier, I realized that this was a national problem. I concluded that these problems can be dealt with only in their proper context: the new world of work and the new economic world order. One is inextricably linked with the other.

The new international arena is one of economic competition, and the winners will be those who can perform the new "smart work" best. And the best workers, I concluded, are those who have received the best training.

I began by looking out on the world from the state-house, but what I found led me, in the end, back to the schoolhouse.

There, to my dismay, I discovered that the majority of our institutions of learning were so far out of touch with the reality of the new world of work that our young people were in effect being schooled for yesterday, not tomorrow.

The system was not working because government, business, and education were out of sync. Government had not yet acknowledged the seriousness of the problem. Education was adapting too slowly to change. And business was pursuing its natural instinct for self-interest.

It became increasingly clear to me that the responsibility of confronting this problem lies with the nation as a whole, and its elected representatives in particular. We all have to learn what it takes to survive and to thrive in a world of tough competition and dizzying change.

5

A Revolution Is Needed

A ND NOW I would like to propose a revolution.
Like any revolution — and I include the one that
gave birth to this nation — this one begins with ideas on
how to create a better society. Any thoughtful person
looking honestly at our schools, our labor force, and
our society as a whole will soon conclude that something has gone awry and that new ideas are needed to
improve the situation. Yet we all know that it is not
likely to get better without concerted thought and action by those experienced enough to take the long view
and bold enough to seize the day.

The relationship between the United States' basic
institutions — school, workplace, and government —
must be woven into a new pattern. Where there has
been isolation, there must now be direct communication. Where there has been suspicion and distance, there
now must be trust and close cooperation. And where
there has been benign neglect, there must now be im-
partial analysis and swift action.

The schools are the point where change will occur first. They are the fulcrum of progress in this new world, where a first-class education is no longer a civilized luxury but an instrument of economic survival. Business will have to make certain modifications. And government must also hear our clarion call for change. But it is the schools that will have to introduce the most far-reaching changes. Not only will what they teach and how they are organized have to be reassessed, but their role in our society will need a thorough reappraisal.

Incremental change will not be enough. Bold ideas are needed. We need twenty-first-century thinking to meet the educational needs of twenty-first-century society. And in our high schools a new American youth apprenticeship system is a good place for our youth to start facing the challenges of the new century. Indeed, there is a built-in incentive for students to participate in this new American approach to secondary education: the business community will hire its participants. If schools are the fulcrum for reform, then a nationwide youth apprenticeship system is the lever. Youth apprenticeship meets the needs of many of our high-school-age students — particularly those who want to combine their academic schoolwork with on-site skill training.

Jobs for the Future (JFF), founded in 1983 and based in Boston, Massachusetts, conducts research, provides technical assistance, and proposes policy innovation on the interrelated issues of workforce development, economic development, and learning reform. Its goal is to encourage policies and practices that prepare all citizens for lives of productive work and learning.

JFF defines youth apprenticeship as a learning program for students aged sixteen and older integrating on-the-job learning with classroom instruction; bridging high school and postsecondary schooling; and resulting in both academic credentials and certification of mastery of workplace skills.

To prepare workers for jobs in construction and manufacturing, there have long been "registered apprenticeships" programs in this country. These programs train and certify young adults for employment. However, these apprenticeships have been very limited in scope; only about 5 percent of high-school graduates enroll, and only about a fifth of those stick with it for the full three years. The trade union involved, usually in coordination with a hiring company, oversees these registered apprenticeships and sets, in cooperation with the U.S. Department of Labor, the stringent certification requirements.

Typically, participants in registered apprenticeships have been out of high school for some time. In an effort to get younger people interested, and to provide them with more educational options, "preapprenticeships" have recently been established. This is a route that can lead to both a journey worker certificate and the potential for an associate degree. The multiyear course involves part-time work in the chosen field during high school. After graduation, this becomes full-time work in the registered apprenticeship, in addition to technical college enrollment in related courses.

While registered apprenticeships certainly have their place, youth apprenticeship is intended to serve a much larger percentage of students. It is similar to the

European models, where apprenticeships date back centuries in Germany and Austria, decades in Denmark. Up to 60 percent of students in some European nations begin their work lives through a rigorous combination of paid work and academic learning. These programs have evolved over time, shaping themselves to fit each country's economy and social climate. We here in the United States should take a good, hard look at some of the elements that have worked in Europe, and then have the good sense to apply them stateside:

- Cooperation and communication between schools, employers, labor, and all levels of government.
- Portable, universally recognized certification of skills mastery and academic achievement.
- Integration of the academic and work-based aspects of apprenticeship.
- A clearly defined, readily available system that reaches a significant percentage of young people.
- A variety of high-wage, high-skill career options that do not require a four-year college degree.

Because youth apprenticeship is still new in the United States, no single model has yet won broad acceptance. There is consensus, however, on the basic elements that differentiate it from less intensive models linking school and work.

Since 1990, Jobs for the Future has focused increasingly on its National Youth Apprenticeship Initiative, which has worked at the local, state, and national levels to study and assist new models for linking school and work for young people. JFF identifies the key design elements as follows:

1. Employers provide paid work experience and guided learning opportunities at the worksite. Paid work experience is at the heart of youth apprenticeship, with the apprentice moving through progressively higher quality jobs during a multiyear program. Through formal training, workplace training, and mentoring by fellow workers, participants learn the skills integral to the worksite.

2. Academic and vocational learning at school are well integrated. Youth apprenticeship is a brand of education reform, and it breaks down barriers between academic and vocational learning. Apprentices are taught to high academic standards, often accomplished through team teaching, project-based instruction, and other instructional innovation.

3. School and workplace learning are coordinated. Instruction at one location reinforces the other through regular interaction, consultation, and planning between workplace and school personnel.

4. Programs include high school and postsecondary learning and last at least two years. Youth apprenticeship creates a strong bridge between high school and postsecondary opportunities — crucially important to young people and parents, according to a JFF study. Most models specify that postsecondary credits and certificates should be transferable to four-year academic programs.

5. Those who complete the program receive widely rec-

ognized credentials of both academic and occupational skill mastery. Successful youth apprentices receive a certificate attesting to the skills learned, based upon qualifications established by the industry. The certificate is generally in addition to the high-school diploma and any postsecondary degree or qualification.

6. Programs are governed by broad coalitions of institutional partners, including high schools, employers, workers and their unions (where applicable), postsecondary institutions, community groups, and government.

This set of basic elements distinguishes youth apprenticeship from other, more traditional school-to-work efforts in the country. I believe these elements also help youth apprenticeship leverage the most economic opportunity from our education system.

As Professor Stephen Hamilton of Cornell University writes in his book *Apprenticeship for Adulthood:*

> With patience and thoughtful reflection, we can reinvent apprenticeship. . . . [This] will challenge the capacity of schools, communities, workplaces, and government to work together to create new learning environments for youth. Not accepting the challenge will condemn growing proportions of young people to the margins of society, where they will threaten our stability and prosperity, even our survival. Creating new avenues to adulthood will enable them to achieve their highest aspirations and to

contribute their energy and talents to the common good.

Youth apprenticeship is quite simply the best way for our country to prepare for the imminent arrival of the twenty-first century. We can either enter into that future with a good head of steam or go in coughing and sputtering. As always, the choice is ours. One way or another, the choice will be made. I propose we show some courage and make the right one.

There are two reasons why a nationwide youth apprenticeship system is the best solution to what currently ails our economy and our society. First, the very implementation of such a system requires that education, business, and government form a dynamic, creative partnership. Second, the products of that system — generation after generation of highly skilled workers unmatched in the world — will supply us with the energy and force to surge ahead through the century to come.

Revolutions are spurred by problems that are causing real pain. We've got plenty of those. But criticism without solutions is nothing but empty carping.

There is an old Maine story about the tourist coming across the bridge between New Hampshire and Maine. When he arrives on the Maine side of the bridge, he comes to a fork in the road. Route 1 goes to the right and the access road to Interstate 95 goes to the left. A sign in the middle says "Portland," with arrows pointing both to the left and to the right. A confusing sign, needless to say, so the tourist asks a fellow who lives in a house by the road, "Does it make any difference which road I take to Portland?" To which the Mainer curtly answers, "Not to me it don't!"

As residents of a popular tourist destination, we in Maine don't care which road people take to get here — we just want them to come! In terms of the direction our country takes in reforming its education system, however, the road we pick will make an enormous difference. In fact, I would suggest that our future standard of living depends on our making the right choice.

As a governor, it is my duty to tackle the problems of my state; as a citizen, it is my duty to share what I have learned with the rest of the country. The following is my Top Ten list of what is required to prepare our young people for the world of work, which is, after all, where they will spend at least forty years of their lives.

McKernan's Top Ten Lessons Learned

1. *Everybody needs somebody.* All students need a mentor — someone who will stay with them throughout the years of their education to help them overcome obstacles, provide experienced guidance, and motivate them to succeed. These are, after all, young people. What works best of all is when that adult takes personal responsibility for a student's success.

2. *If you haven't got a skill, you won't get a good job.* Skills sell. It's that simple: if you have a valued skill, you will get a good job. All the demographic data described elsewhere in this book makes a compelling case that skills will be the essential factor in an indi-

vidual's ability to have a good job, take care of a family, and support a rewarding lifestyle.

3. *Business must be clear about what it wants.* In every successful program I have encountered, the strategies that work are the ones in which business has clearly defined the skills people need.

4. *Young people need to know why they are getting educated.* Survey after survey demonstrates that young people who have no clue about what they are going to do with their lives are the ones most likely to drop out of school, get bad grades, or become discipline problems. Those with focused goals are the ones who succeed.

5. *Keep government out of the way.* Government should enable young people, schools, and businesses to conduct programs that they jointly agree upon and will take responsibility for — and then get out of the way.

   I want to repeat the key point of the last statement — educators can't do it alone. And they shouldn't. It takes business, educators, and young people — supported by their parents and appropriate mentors — to have a truly effective strategy leading to a good job.

6. *"The best social program ever devised is a job."* I always admired Ronald Reagan's ability to state, in simple terms, some fundamental truths. The statement above is one of them. Good jobs will result in dramatic spending reductions for many of our social ills — broken homes, child and spouse abuse, a lack of health care coverage, and the spirit-crushing cycle of welfare dependency. Let's consider for a moment

what would happen if everyone had a job paying forty thousand dollars or more, a likely wage level for those with salable skills. What would it mean for the ability of our citizens to live the American dream? Think how our national spirit would soar. Americans are a kind and generous people, and the suffering of our fellow citizens drags us all down.

7. *Measure the results in real terms.* Save the fluff. Every training or educational strategy needs to have a bottom line. In this case, the bottom line is the ability of young people to secure and keep a good job based on the skills they received from their education.

8. *Recognize competency from both a business and an educational perspective.* A high-school diploma or an associate's degree doesn't tell the full story. Business must define the skills it needs, but it must also recognize the workers who meet or exceed these skills and have credentials to prove it.

9. *Hold someone accountable.* A lesson we should all have learned is the fundamental value of holding people and organizations responsible for results. Nowhere is accountability more important than in preparing young people well for their future.

10. *If something works, apply it and expand it. If it doesn't, fix it or end it.* All of us in public policy positions, and specifically in education, have tolerated recurring failure, mediocrity, and outright waste for far too long. We have to be much, much tougher — and unforgiving. One student's future is more important than any "special interest" defending its consistent failures in order to protect its self-serving status quo.

Youth Apprenticeship Works

The potential of youth apprenticeship as the solution to the United States' social and economic problems has already been recognized to a considerable extent at the grassroots level — a multitude of programs can be found in nearly every state of the union. The rub is that these efforts have been uncoordinated, haphazard, sometimes shortsighted, and oftentimes timid.

Indeed, although the transition from school to work has been on the front burner at the U.S. Department of Labor for a decade, only recently has the issue come to the fore in the national debate. Secretaries of labor, from Bill Brock and Ann McLaughlin in the Reagan administration, to Elizabeth Dole and Lynn Martin in the Bush administration, to Robert Reich in the Clinton administration, have all presented compelling arguments for a national youth apprenticeship system. But still, the nation has been slow to heed their call.

We need national leadership to pull it all together.

The obvious remedy of apprenticeship has been acknowledged by schools, unions, and business. Unions alone have some forty-three thousand programs to better a worker's skills. These programs, though, are designed for adults and are not connected to the education of our children.

Likewise, businesses crave a nationwide system that will ensure well-skilled, productive workers — and that will stand behind their training and education. Bill Kolberg, president of the National Alliance of Business, argues for this sort of portable training credential in his recent book, *Rebuilding America's Workforce*:

> Certification allows portability, an important asset for workers and employers alike in a nation with as mobile a workforce as the United States.
>
> The U.S. needs a national certification program for a broad range of frontline workers' skills. Businesses need assurance that new workers have been trained to world-class standards. . . . As the business community leads the way in developing definitions for needed skills, it can also take advantage of the activities already under way in this area.

There is a similar lack of connection in all of the other various programs now in place. Technical institutes and community colleges provide some of the training, but the average age of their students is twenty-nine. Something like a million students enroll in cooperative education programs in high school and two-year colleges. Though in some ways similar to apprenticeship programs, "co-ops," as they are known, suffer from a lack of accepted standards, and the school-employer arrangements are strictly local. School-based enterprises — restaurants, print shops, auto repair shops, construction programs, and so on — aim to improve preparation but without any real connection to the business they're aiming for. The same problems are to be found in the tech-prep movement, which, although providing a technology-based vocational education, tends to be entirely school-driven and doesn't offer on-site training for those seeking work-based learning.

Numerous as these programs are, they still represent only a small fraction of the population. The figures speak for themselves. In 1989 the United States had only 263,000 registered apprentices, a mere 2 percent of U.S. high-school graduates. Treasury secretary Lloyd Bentsen has said, "I asked a German industrialist [Germany boasts a very advanced training program for its young people] if you just had to settle for one thing that gave you a competitive edge against the rest of the nations of the world . . . what would it be? He said, 'Our apprenticeship program.' "

A report issued during the Bush administration by the Department of Education, "Youth Apprenticeship, American Style," summarized a conference held in December 1990 and attended by 350 representatives of business, labor, nonprofit organizations, government, and education. That report notes: "The United States is not alone among the industrialized nations in facing [stiff] economic competition from low-wage developing nations. But it *is* alone in facing that competition with a poorly trained workforce." The report quotes Professor Hamilton as saying, "Virtually all of our competitors have something like the German apprenticeship system; only the United States has nothing."

It is when students first begin the work-based learning of an apprenticeship that it becomes clear how such a program differs from our traditional school-to-work approach. An apprenticeship program is established by education and business working together. Together they plan a program that takes account of available jobs and what skills are needed to fill these jobs. Once the necessary skills have been identified, both the school and the employers decide what students will learn in the workplace and what will be taught in school. Generally, the student will spend as much time studying outside the classroom as in it.

Christopher Cross, executive director of the Business Roundtable Education Initiative and former assistant secretary of education for educational research and improvement, expressed this truth quite clearly: "Watching and imitating is how children make their way into adulthood . . . apprenticing youngsters to masters is founded on this fact of life." The apprenticeship program emerges from the very nature of human life.

We can no longer compete by relying on the out-of-date mass production techniques of the past. Our service industries, too, call for good analytical abilities, teamwork, and problem-solving capabilities. European apprenticeship programs emphasize these skills.

A technological revolution has already occurred in the world of work, and another is under way in the United States' response to that new world. In essence, all we must now do is to finish what's already been started — but finish it with due deliberation and intelligence, not to mention the old Yankee sense of what works.

Though we have begun to respond, we are still making fundamental errors. Tests worldwide indicate that students graduating from the best colleges — Harvard, Oxford, the Sorbonne, the University of Tokyo, or Heidelberg — are roughly equivalent in learning and performance. It is the remaining population — the large majority — that makes the vital difference in a country's productivity. By focusing our attention on the college-bound, we have essentially been paying the greatest attention to those who need it least, and the least attention to those who need it most. That may have been fine for the past. It is not for the future. We have a current education system that gives our future managers and professionals special nurturing in their last years of high school. The needs of the others, who will form the nation's labor force, aren't viewed as sufficient to warrant the outlay of time and money.

Yet common sense tells us that if airplane wing bolts fall out, it's not the CEO's fault or even the designer's, but probably the worker who was supposed to tighten them. And a doctor's decision to operate or not will only be as good as the information she receives from lab technicians. Close to 70 percent of U.S. jobs don't require a four-year college degree. They require superb basic training. The secret to productivity is a skilled workforce. The secret to a skilled workforce is an education that prepares students for the realities of work. And the secret of that kind of an education is improved communication and cooperation between U.S. business and education.

The communication has to happen first. And there are plenty of obstacles to it, on both sides. Educators fear "vocationalization." But, upon examination, that fear proves groundless. Fifty, forty, even thirty years ago, teachers would have had some basis for those apprehensions. In the old world of work, with its narrow parameters, vocationalization was a real concern because it was a real possibility. But today, and tomorrow, in a world of work transformed by computers and electronic communication, that fear is simply out of date.

It is often forgotten in discussions of youth apprenticeship that providing the student with a marketable skill is only half the battle. Just as important, perhaps even more so, is training the student for "lifetime learning," the mental flexibility required to keep pace with the speed of change. The skill a student learns in a youth apprenticeship program could easily be obsolete in ten or fifteen years. That student's continued prosperity will then depend on his or her ability to acquire new skills quickly and competently.

It turns out that the basics, the three R's, have acquired renewed importance in the new economic context. Students must have mastered language and basic mathematics in order to function at the level required by today's world of work. Communication skills are universally acknowledged to be essential in this age of instant communication, and math is the obvious stepping-stone to computer literacy.

We may be producing a generation of Nintendo experts, but if they can't read a training manual, how will they apply what they know about computers to the workplace? It may sound old-fashioned, but no amount of vocational education can make up for the lack of a thorough grasp of the basic skills taught in the elementary grades. Recent studies have found that almost half of adult Americans can't even write a short letter explaining a problem on a credit-card bill. The 1993 Goals Panel Report also found that only 52 percent of American adults have mastered sufficient literary skills to be able to perform effectively in the modern economy. That statistic adds up to almost half of our population. The report goes on to point out that lacking such essential qualifications, half our population "cannot perform the range of complex literacy tasks [that are] important for competing successfully in a global economy and exercising fully the rights and responsibilities of citizenship."

Real-World Examples

This is a frightening fact. It is one that needs to be addressed. A well-structured youth apprenticeship program will speak to these needs — it can't afford not to. At a pilot program in Boston called Project ProTech, high-school students are trained in various occupations, among them medical technician. The program has created some notable success stories. Two young women spent a year in the histology lab at Deaconess Hospital and at the end of that period, according to their supervisor, were as competent as most members of the regular staff. These are students who a couple of years earlier might have settled for a counter job with McDonald's; they might even have dropped out of high school. What's changed? Their self-esteem and their real chances for a better life have increased. Exciting, isn't it?

We see that educators shouldn't fear youth apprenticeship but rather welcome it as an opportunity to renew their fundamental mission: preparing the young for life.

Once students become interested in one form of work, they often respond by working harder at other forms.

Matt Burr, a Maine student, was a sophomore at Gorham High School. He was taking general courses and, by his own admission, was only an "OK student. I wasn't that great in English." After working for a year for D&G Machine in Westbrook, Matt's outlook on school changed, thanks to his youth apprenticeship program. As he reported, "I am now getting A's in Advanced English."

More evidence of the contribution of apprenticeship programs to academic performance comes from Tammy Wheeler, who was a student at Westbrook High School. Before entering her apprenticeship at Maine Medical Center, Tammy had taken nothing but general courses. After working with brain-injured patients and helping those with other disabilities, Tammy was prompted to switch from general courses to algebra, anatomy, and other subjects that, she said, "are going to help me. I want to go to college and become a physical therapy assistant. You need a lot of anatomy and algebra."

Parents have fears of another sort. They worry that a youth apprenticeship program is in fact a form of "tracking," separating the college-bound from those who will go directly from high school into the workforce. But isn't that, in fact, what occurs anyway? Don't we already separate the college-bound to make sure they receive everything they need in the way of guidance and counseling? The percentage who don't go on to college, not to mention the 20 percent who fail to finish high school, are simply left to fend for themselves. As a result, we are left with unskilled graduates and appalling statistics. Each statistic is a personal human tragedy — a story of drug abuse, crime, teenage pregnancy, and unemployment. Rather than "tracking," the youth apprenticeship program I propose includes one year of college, with easy access for those who want to continue on for associate or baccalaureate degrees. Those are the options and career pathways all young people need.

Parents also worry that sixteen-year-olds (the age at which students would enter a youth apprenticeship program) aren't equipped to make sensible career choices. But under the current system, aren't choices being made by default? Aren't far too many students choosing to tune out or drop out at precisely this stage in their education? Moreover, a properly designed youth apprenticeship program opens new vistas to students and leads them to a reevaluation of their own future. No one would be locked into only one direction. Those who are still uncertain will have the freedom to move between college-prep classes and youth apprenticeship. And the program will also be open to those who are college-bound but want the insurance policy of having mastered a skill or set of skills. Once it becomes apparent to parents, students, and employers that apprenticeship produces graduates who are well educated and well paid, doubts will disappear quickly.

Business Involvement Needed

Odd as it may seem, it is not parents, students, educators, or even those in government who pose the most

significant and stubborn opposition to a youth apprenticeship program, but rather the sector of society that
is most likely to benefit directly from it: business. Two
fundamental attitudes are at work here: one is based on
real — and unfortunate — experience, and the other on
a misreading of the possibilities.

Business sees that schools are preparing young
people who are educated but unskilled at best, or uneducated and unskilled at worst. For example, Baldor
Electric, an Arkansas electronics firm, introduced new
manufacturing technologies with complexity that
proved insurmountable for too many of its workers. Of
those who volunteered to be tested, more than half
could not read at all or had reading skills that were
below eighth-grade level. Not only are these products
of U.S. education lacking in the basic skills; they are
also deficient in the intangible but essential qualities of
motivation, discipline, and work ethic.

Business can't be faulted for reacting negatively to
these facts. Business can, however, be faulted for draw-
ing a series of erroneous conclusions based both on the
low quality of the workforce and on their projections
of the shape of the future. The response of many U.S.
companies has been to reduce their dependence on full-
time workers by hiring part-timers who receive lower
wages and no benefits, to expect less of their employees,
and to replace them altogether with machines. In a
Grant Thornton survey of 250 midsize manufacturing
companies, most respondents felt no need to upgrade
their workers' skills. The consensus among business
seems to be that there are plenty of skilled workers
around — a situation created by the fact that many have

been thrown out of work by automation and are seeking jobs. Former labor secretary William E. Brock, co-chair of the Commission on the Skills in the American Workforce, summed it up: "The good news is that there is no skills shortage. This is also the bad news."

What it comes down to is a real lack of foresight on the part of U.S. business. Obviously we can't compete with most of the world on wages, and as the rest of the world catches up with our manufacturing technology, their quality will match ours. What can we do to stay in the game? A Jobs for the Future youth apprenticeship conference report is unflinching: "Faced with the impossibility of producing cheaper, American firms must compete by producing *smarter* — improving product quality more rapidly, introducing new products more frequently, and customizing products to meet the needs of narrow market niches."

Even European businesses see the potential of American youth apprenticeship. Albert Hoser, president and CEO of the American subsidiary of German multinational Siemens Corporation, in discussing its American plant apprenticeships, says, "Our productivity and ultimate success depend upon unlocking the full capability of our entire workforce. . . . We see apprenticeship training and all employee education as empowering and enriching our employees."

In the years to come those people who are educated, skilled, and flexible and are able to create, apply, and repair the latest technologies will make the difference between economies that flourish and those that flounder. Establishing a youth apprenticeship system will be the beginning of a long-term effort to ensure that future workers coming out of our schools have the education and skills to enhance the American economy.

Some will point out that U.S. workers are still number one in productivity. But their very use of the word *still* indicates an uneasy sense that the competition is closing in. The statistics support that uneasiness. Although there are recent signs of improvement, the productivity of the U.S. worker in the private, nonagricultural sector has been increasing at the rate of only 1 percent a year over the last fifteen years. In Europe it has grown 3.5 percent. In Japan the growth rate is 6 percent, and in the newly industrialized nations of Asia, a staggering 10 percent increase has been recorded. It can be argued that these nations, especially those of the Pacific Rim, have shown such dramatic improvement precisely because there was so much room for improvement. But that smacks of self-satisfaction.

The United States' past greatness is a guide, not a guarantee. The past tells us that though many economic and social problems can be solved, there are also others, like the Manhattan Project and the exploration of space, that require a high level of organization and the mobilization of a great array of energy and expertise. The disparate and uncoordinated nature of the many youth apprenticeship programs that have proliferated only serves to prove that coordination at the national level is essential. If we institute a national youth apprenticeship system, we will produce students who have the confidence of well-prepared workers, their abilities certified by future employers whose standards are known to be exacting. These students can go off into the working world certain that their skills are needed because they've been developed in concert with the very people who will be paying them.

And if we fail to institute this new system, the whole country will be paying — in lost jobs, lost income, and lost exports. The competition will continue to get better in some countries and cheaper in others. But the greatest loss will be the loss of hope and faith in the generations of Americans to come.

Youth apprenticeship, then, is not just a way of improving education and the workforce; it is a fundamental choice that the United States has to make. It is a choice of direction but also a choice of identity. Who do we want to be, and what kind of society do we want to create? The choice lies between selfish apathy and concerted action.

There are real problems in the United States today, and stiff challenges from the rest of the world. We must show that late-twentieth-century Americans have the courage to face facts, the will to take charge, and the ingenuity to find solutions.

To the generations of Americans yet to come, we owe a revolution in the way we care for our young people. We owe a revolution at the close of the twentieth century to the people who launched our first one by writing the Declaration of Independence and the Constitution, and by fighting to make the United States free.

We owe it to ourselves.

6

What the Competition Is Doing

HOW DO WE KNOW we can change our educational system? Are other countries doing a better job preparing their young people for the modern world? Do their children finish school better equipped than our youth to find well-paying jobs? Many European countries, and Japan as well, have well-trained and highly skilled workforces. What part did their schools play in this achievement? How do they differ from our schools? In 1991, I decided to set out to examine their educational systems and to see if I could find some answers there.

I had been to Japan in 1986, to learn what I could from their celebrated success with a productive workforce. To my surprise, it wasn't their vaunted "corporation as family" that struck me most. Instead, I found myself impressed by the close alliance between education and industry. Japanese companies know that schools are training their most valuable asset — their future workers — and that something of such importance cannot be left to chance. I had the impression that Japanese businesses treat schools with the same care and respect that they accord to all their suppliers.

The point was made clear at one of the Nissan plants. After demonstrating how robotics is used to construct cars, one manager explained that without the focus in schools on the educational needs of future workers, the company would never have been able to get the most out of this advanced technology.

I visited a Japanese school and saw for myself the discipline and hard work for which the country is famous. Mothers told us that they spent as much time as necessary to make sure that their children did well in school. I heard of schoolboys getting up at dawn on Saturday morning to play — before attending a half day of classes. I knew, and they knew, that every one of those Saturday hours would eventually lead to money in the bank.

At my meeting with Japan's Ministry of International Trade and Industry, one of the ministers said that Japan's economic success has been driven, in large part, by having the "best bottom-half workforce in the world." The educated elite of any country are more or less equal in intelligence, education, and ability. The cutting edge advantage comes in the "bottom half" — not executives then, but the blue-collar workers.

I gained some valuable insights during that trip, but I realized the answers to our problems couldn't be found there. The differences between U.S. and Japanese society are too great — not only in culture and attitude, in history and civilization, but also in geography and population. Japan is a small island nation with a homogeneous population of 118 million. We are an enormous country with a diverse population of 250 million.

Europe's Model

Europe would clearly be a better resource for change. It is a commonly accepted fact that Germany, and some of the other European nations as well, does a first-rate job of preparing technicians for the workforce. So, in January 1992, thanks to the financial support of the German Marshall Fund, I led a delegation from Jobs for America's Graduates to Europe to examine their approach. I wanted to see for myself how they handle their training, how it differs from ours, and, most of all, I wanted to find out what we could learn from them. Although I had read many reports and studies before I left, I still wasn't prepared for the telling differences between their systems and ours. The trip turned out to be an enlightening, sobering, and inspiring experience.

As soon as we landed in Munich, I could see that the city had been able to integrate the past with present, all the while keeping an eye on the future. From the fifteenth-century Frauenkirche to the modern training facilities at BMW, it was clear that Germany had found a way to blend its past with the needs of a new global economy.

Germany is committed to an educational system that emphasizes training students in technological skills. To implement this policy, they combine academic studies with exacting courses in vocational and apprentice training. The country's constitution spells it out: "To provide each individual with high-quality academic and vocational training commensurate with his/her abilities and interests and to continue to make opportunities for personal, occupational and political education available to him/her throughout his/her life." And, as I discovered, the Germans adhere to the letter of this law. They keep their promises. They mean business.

German youth must complete three levels of schooling: primary, which begins at age six; secondary, at age ten; and upper-secondary school, at age sixteen. All students follow the same curriculum through the first five years: a course of study demanding high levels of achievement in mathematics, language, basic history, science, and the arts. Those who have difficulty are given extra help immediately.

At the age of ten, each student is channeled into one of three levels of secondary education. The decision is made by student, parents, and teachers, and determines what kind of further education that child will receive. The three levels are: *Hauptschule,* basic education for those who don't intend to go on to a university or higher levels of vocational training; *Realschule,* general education mixed with some practical training, which prepares students for nonprofessional jobs or specialized technical schools; and *Gymnasium,* equivalent to our academic high school.

Students who are destined to go to universities attend a *Gymnasium.* Both *Hauptschule* and *Realschule* lead to vocational training. During these years, roughly ages ten to sixteen, the first steps are taken to introduce students to practical work. Through field trips and "work shadowing," children follow a production process. At an early age, they begin to grasp the connection between what they're learning and how they will, in time, make a living. As they know their options, older students can make well-thought-out decisions about their future.

By exposing them early to different occupations, Germany encourages young people to think seriously about what they want to be and do later on. Students are not only prepared for the future, but, by their teenage years, they understand the vital link between learning and vocation. They see that the school and the factory dovetail dynamically, that they work together as a single entity, one which puts knowledge to practical use. The students don't have to be told this: they live it.

As students progress through the grades, the workplace becomes increasingly significant. Employers and labor-market specialists visit schools and talk to students about the choicest jobs and what they must do to get them.

This policy of career preparation is not unique to Germany. Scandinavian students complete nine years of compulsory schooling, from age seven to sixteen. In their educational systems, Denmark and Sweden also stress the importance of work experience outside the school.

In Denmark, eighth- and ninth-graders are exposed to practical work through a week's employment in an actual business. This initial foray into the working world is made possible by the collaboration of schools, community service organizations, and parents. Students also meet with the school's career counselors both in class and one on one. Such an emphasis on career training amounts to nothing more than common sense. Here are youngsters who will grow up and have to make a living for at least forty years. It is certainly worth spending time and money to prepare them.

The Swedes begin even earlier than the Danes. In the first three years of school, children learn about the workplace through field trips and shadowing their parents at their jobs. This exposure increases as students move up through the grades. Before they finish their compulsory schooling, Swedish students must complete between six and ten weeks of practical work, usually with a local firm. The Swedish government subsidizes the participating companies.

The telling difference, I discovered, between our educational system and the systems in Germany and Scandinavia, lies in the value these countries put on learning by doing. Vocational training and youth apprenticeship programs are an integral part of schooling, not an extracurricular activity, often treated, in our schools, as poor and unwelcome relations.

Germans have developed a "dual system" of education, one which coordinates academic work and youth apprenticeship programs. At the end of compulsory schooling, 25 percent of the students go on to higher education and 10 percent drop out and become part of the unskilled workforce. By far the largest number of students — nearly two thirds — enters the dual system, the name for Germany's program of youth apprenticeships. These students continue their academic education, but at the same time they focus on practical work. Until the age of eighteen, all students must take at least part-time vocational training.

Once German students decide to enter the dual apprenticeship program, they are made responsible for finding a firm that will train them. Participation is strictly voluntary, and not all firms take part. Companies receive no incentive to establish a training program. Although only 20 percent of all German firms take in apprentices, all the major industrial firms — who employ 80 percent of the German workforce — are involved. In 1992, these companies trained more than a million and a half apprentices.

It is significant that a number of *Gymnasium* students enroll in the apprenticeship programs before entering the university. They are taking no chances — they want to make sure they have at least one marketable skill that can earn them a living.

I was made aware of the value of apprenticeship programs during a dinner in Munich with a leading banker. He told me that applicants at his bank who had gone through an apprenticeship in banking and then earned a university degree are among the most sought-after new employees: obviously these students understand what a banking career entails and have made it their first choice.

All German businesses are members of either the Chamber of Trade and Craft or the Chamber of Industry and Commerce. These bodies, which represent both employers and employees, ensure that certain training guidelines are followed. Small companies pay dues of about fifty dollars a year, and large companies pay from

6 to 10 percent of their annual corporate tax. Companies pay these dues whether they are training apprentices or not. The money is used to administer apprenticeship programs and to assist small firms that do not have the facilities to meet training requirements. For example, an apprentice may be training for a position as a clerk in a local bank that doesn't handle international accounts. To learn about international transactions, the student is sent to a local training center or to another city where banks do international business. The programs thus make certain that all apprentices in a particular trade receive the same basic training.

While German apprentices train, they receive an allowance equivalent to 20 to 25 percent of the full wage paid a journeyman worker. This averages five hundred to eight hundred dollars a month.

Since German companies bear these costs themselves — which in 1992 averaged more than ten thousand dollars per apprenticeship — there's a real inducement to get a student trained and on the job. Yet, despite these costs, German companies continue to train. Why? Because they know it is a small price to pay for training the labor they will eventually employ.

A federal mandate establishes a detailed curriculum for the apprentice programs and outlines the legal relationship between teacher and apprentice, clarifying their respective rights and obligations. The mandate ensures that certain minimum standards are met. Training hours and vacation time are regulated as well; so, too, are the skills to be acquired, the examinations to be passed, the minimum requirements to be met by an apprentice, and a rough timetable for the program.

Germany is determined, says Dr. Herman Schmidt, the secretary-general of the Federal Institute of Vocational Education, to remain a first-class world power in the postindustrial age. There will be, he said, a new emphasis on service industries such as communications, planning, control, research, and teaching. The Germans believe in a well-informed workforce. Employers continually report on government labor policies and employer needs in a changing economy — all closely coordinated with their vocational education system.

The Danes, too, emphasize general schooling combined with apprentice training. On my very first night in Copenhagen, I was given a living illustration of the Danes' acknowledgment of the connection between work and education. I was having dinner in our hotel dining room with John Fitzsimmons, president of the Maine Technical College System, when we noticed that the young man serving our table wore a tag reading "Apprentice Waiter." Naturally, we questioned him. He told us that he had already finished a chef's apprenticeship, but, because he hoped someday to manage or own a restaurant, he had decided on a second apprenticeship in the dining room.

In Denmark, as in Germany, all firms pay into a general fund administered by labor and employers. The money is divided among those companies that accept apprentices to offset the cost of training wages. A student in the third year of training receives 65 percent of the wage he or she will earn when the apprenticeship is over. (Germans contend that by paying such high wages, Danes decrease students' incentive to fulfill their obligations.) By requiring all companies to pay into the training fund, Danish authorities hope to increase employer participation.

When we met with the officers of Novo Nordisk, a pharmaceutical company that provides apprenticeship training to 138 young workers, we were given further insights into the program. The head of the company's training program believes that the success of Danish apprenticeship rests on a firm, three-way understanding among employers, schools, and students.

As an example, he told the story of an apprentice whom the company found deficient in math. The solution was simple. The company informed the school, and the young man was given extra math courses during his next stint in school. When he returned six months later, much improved in mathematics, he found that new apprenticeship opportunities had opened up for him.

Bertel Haarder, then Denmark's minister of education, is convinced that many students are thoroughly sick of traditional schooling by the time they have finished tenth grade. Apprenticeship opens up an attractive new path to learning and to future jobs.

In Denmark, apprentices are often trained by small firms and then go on to work for larger companies. But the small business incurs no loss. Apprentices benefit from training in small firms because they get experience in a wider array of jobs than they would in a large concern, where the needs for specialization are greater. Small companies pay nothing, apprentices acquire a broader range of skills, and big business gains a well-trained workforce. A win-win situation if ever there was one.

Sweden takes a different approach. At vocational schools, students train for a set number of years in a particular trade, but on-the-job training is less common there. There are no exams, practical or written. Apprentices are awarded a certificate for completing a program, not for demonstrating aptitude. A prospective employer has no way of judging a worker's ability. The Swedes have recognized the weakness of their approach and are now moving toward the German model.

In Germany, I also learned that many companies, to meet their technological needs, actually go far beyond legal training requirements. At one factory that I visited, an apprentice welder was practicing with a high-speed, digitally computerized cutting torch. Learning how to use this equipment wasn't required for his certificate. But it makes sense from the company's point of view: better training makes better workers. Training in Germany doesn't focus on one job in one plant. Apprentices are given broad-based instruction, which will allow them to use several skills in a given field. It makes them flexible and adaptable — essential qualities in a world that demands constant change.

I was surprised to learn that German companies are under no obligation to hire the apprentices that they have trained, and apprentices don't have to go to work for the companies, either. Why, I asked, are these firms willing to pay for training? I was told that 90 percent of trainees remain with the same firm or go back to that firm after getting more education.

Most apprenticeship programs in Germany run for two or three years. A typical workweek consists of three or four days of work with a company, and one or two days in a local vocational school. Some of the larger firms have schools on site. We visited one such training center at the Siemens Company. It has more than five hundred trainees each year in ten different industrial and technical occupations. I was impressed, while watching students being instructed in the procedure for bending metal, to see that a teacher was at the same time writing down the formulas relating to the stress capabilities of that type of metal. Now this was education with an impact. This kind of applied learning establishes a connection for the student between the practical and the theoretical. These apprentices not only absorb a lesson in a mechanical procedure but also learn the basic physics that underlies the practice. We don't do that in the United States.

Trainers are carefully chosen. They are craftspeople, not just older employees taken off the assembly line. They are given extensive training in teaching and receive extra pay. When students aren't training, they're in class studying related subjects — the German language, foreign languages, math, and social studies. In addition to acquiring skills valuable in the labor market, the students are learning how to learn. Later, when new skills must be mastered, they will have both specific and general knowledge to draw upon.

In all of Europe there probably are no better educated people than the Irish. The percentage of Irish students who go on to upper level education is the highest in Europe, and the country is 99 percent literate. But chronic unemployment remains a blight and is, ironically, one of the reasons that many students pursue advanced education. But this will change. Even in the midst of these social woes, the Irish have not lost sight of the critical importance of education to their economic survival.

Four different groups contribute to an Irish student's curriculum: the government's Department of Education, universities, teachers' associations, and the business community. Industrial representatives are on board to ensure that courses reflect the world of work. In chemistry, for instance, a committee of educators and businesspeople first draws up a course proposal. Then chemists from major firms review the draft and add suggestions, which are incorporated into the final course.

The greatest growth and change in Irish education, however, is taking place in the nine regional and technical colleges. Attendance at these schools, which have a greater impact on the skills of the workforce than do the universities, has doubled since 1980. Modeled on U.S. junior and community colleges, they offer two-, three-, and four-year programs for apprentices, as well as higher vocational degrees, and part-time and evening courses for adult students.

I heard a story that vividly illustrates the success of Ireland's system. According to the story, at 4:00 A.M., a New York computer operator working the graveyard shift called Quarterdeck Office Systems, a California-based software company with a twenty-four-hour hotline. What he didn't know was that his call was routed not west but east to Dublin, Ireland, where (at 9:00 A.M., Dublin time) a trained specialist was able to solve his problems.

Software companies compete not only through the quality of their product but also through the services they provide. During business hours in the United States, similar calls go to Quarterdeck's customer service department in California. In this case, Quarterdeck was ensuring that customers would receive technological support at any time of day or night.

The lower wages in Ireland more than compensated for the cost of an international call. But, in Ireland, Quarterdeck could also find the specialist able to solve a computer operator's problems. Her education and her training got her the job. It may be flattering but it is also distressing to think that the young Irish woman answering the 800-line for Quarterdeck may have received her education in an institution patterned after one of ours.

In the British Isles, emphasis on education and enhanced skills is not confined simply to Ireland. England and Scotland have also made major efforts at vocational education.

In Britain, most young people have traditionally entered the workforce by age sixteen. In the 1980s, however, traditional career ladders for businesses gave way to the need for higher technical and academic skills. In England and Wales, prime minister Margaret Thatcher created the Youth Training Scheme, a system of subsidies for businesses to hire young people, with the expectation that employers would train the young workers in return. The system was truly employer-driven and may not have adequately monitored student learning and progress.

A lack of adequate follow-through by some businesses resulted in a revised program and the creation of standards in key occupational areas. Most recently, Britain has transferred responsibility for many of its youth-training programs to a system of local businesses called Training and Enterprise Councils (TECs). Britain has established one hundred of these TECs to promote work-based learning and assist with small business development.

Edward Roberts, chief executive of Heath Springs, Ltd., has played a critical role in the development of the TECs, which represent a breakthrough in the Youth Training Scheme because each TEC is locally based and oriented. The TECs administer youth training, but also are charged with examining the local labor market and developing a plan to best meet the training needs of the region. Each TEC works as an independent but quasi-governmental entity, receiving some government funding to administer programs, though still free to adjust the program to meet local needs.

While in England in 1993, I had the opportunity to visit a Sainsbury's Supermarket training program to meet students participating in their Programme for Work Experience. The cross-training and extensive skills youngsters receive at that facility enable them to meet standards accepted throughout the industry.

These standards are developed and monitored by a National Council for Vocational Qualifications, which closely evaluates youth training and provides certification for student trainees. I was impressed with the extensive network of standards developed for the supermarket profession, as well as the extent to which the company tried to make students feel at home.

Although roughly patterned on Britain's youth training, Scotland today offers a distinct system of training for its students. The Scottish system is perhaps most notable for its modular system and standards, which are coordinated by the Scottish Vocational Education Council (SCOTVEC).

By coordinating between national British standards and standards developed by SCOTVEC for Scotland's distinct needs, the system gives students a flexible training system more effective than the English model. Students retain a wider variety of options for a longer period of time, and by combining SCOTVEC modules, they can develop a plan that balances student interests and training needs.

Moreover, the system of Scottish standards is kept up to date through an annual review of the thirty-five hundred training modules. Close to 10 percent of the modules are revised each year in order to take into account teacher suggestions, student experience, and changing employer needs.

The Scottish education system has traditionally coordinated vocational and academic courses, and in 1984 the Scottish Action Plan to integrate and better coordinate its vocational programs was set up. The plan created a versatile system that coordinated secondary school and college courses as well as part-time and full-time work-based learning and apprenticeships.

The plan has replaced most vocational courses

outside of the higher education sector with a system of modules that comprise the students' education. These modules are remarkably distinct from the youth training program in England but link well with the system and effectively tie together the worlds of school and work.

What all the European educational systems have in common is a gradual and practical transition from school to the workplace. Everyone along the way profits: parents, students, teachers, and employers. Parents know their children will be more economically independent and secure. The students know they have skills that can be marketed and the training to adapt to changing conditions. Business and industry get workers who can compete with any in the world.

The primary strength of the apprenticeship program derives from the dynamic cooperation between business and education. The transition from school to job is eased by the removal of guesswork and anxiety. Experience itself proves to students the relevance of their studies. Business can count on new employees who have some knowledge of the world of work. It is only through direct communication with business that educators keep up with changes taking place in industry and commerce.

The European attitude toward vocational training also leads to successful apprenticeship programs. In Europe, where training is thorough and demanding, apprentices meet high standards and pass rigorous exams. Like all well-trained people, students gain confidence and self-esteem, and respect from others.

In medieval days, when very few people were literate, most of the population had to learn by doing. Out of these circumstances grew the powerful medieval guilds, hierarchical organizations that controlled the apprentices, allowing them to progress very gradually to journeyman status and then, perhaps, to master. Europeans, strongly attached to tradition and concerned with the loss of valuable skills through assembly line production, kept the apprenticeship tradition alive and have now adapted it to the most modern of ends. Early immigrants to the United States established a similar system in their new land, but its widespread application failed to survive the Industrial Revolution.

There are many advantages to in-company training as it is practiced in Europe. Students have access to the latest equipment and technologies. Why should government or local schools pay for expensive machinery? The factories must have the current technology to remain competitive. Apprentices also experience problem solving in the workplace. We all know that very little ever goes according to plan. In Europe, students see equipment breaking down or malfunctioning. They learn how to solve problems as part of a group. In European schools, students learn not only by listening to a teacher who stands at the front of the class, but through hands-on teamwork dealing with real and complex problems.

The apprenticeship program is also fueled by the training wages paid to students. There is a promise of higher wages to come. Not only do students enjoy a sense of security about their future employment — they know that their skills and flexibility will grant them upward mobility and the better life for which most people strive. The apprentice is provided with a series of incentives that begin with the training wage and may even end with a shot at directing an entire enterprise. I don't mean to imply that the European economic picture is all rosy. It is not. But one thing they are doing right is preparing their students for the new global workforce.

I left Europe deeply encouraged. I could see weaknesses in their education and training system: it lacked the flexibility needed in the modern economy; the initial training needed to be upgraded to ensure all apprentices would meet world-class standards. But I also saw the wisdom of their approach and how the concepts behind it could help the United States adjust to the experimentation taking place in the school-to-work arena.

Coming back to the United States, I felt I'd found what I'd gone looking for: ideas I could use to change our own system so that in the near future an Irish programmer stuck with a problem might call an 800-line and hear a Midwestern twang, or a "down east" Maine accent, on the other end of the line.

7

The Maine Youth Apprenticeship Program

O N THE TRANSATLANTIC FLIGHT HOME, John Fitzsimmons and I discussed the importance of what we had seen in Europe. European programs were not isolated programs but rather a system for preparing their youth for the world of work. Though Europeans need to adjust their own programs to keep up with the changing economic times, the comprehensive nature of their training is something we can learn from.

Frankly, we are ahead of the Europeans in realizing and responding to the changes in the global economy. We have begun to adapt. What we have never had, however, is a system to address the skill needs of U.S. workers. Around the country, states are beginning to experiment with various approaches to improving the school-to-work transition of young people. Each excels in one particular or another, and each is effective in its own way. In Maine, we were determined to build upon and beyond these American-style reflections of the European systems.

In Tulsa, Oklahoma, in 1992, Craftsmanship 2000, a four-year apprenticeship program in metalworking, was established for both girls and boys in the eleventh grade, starting as a collaborative effort among five groups: local industry, the Tulsa public schools, Tulsa Tech, Tulsa Junior College, and the metropolitan chamber of commerce. The program is run by a not-for-profit corporation based at the chamber of commerce. Craftsmanship 2000 does a masterful job of involving large businesses, and the response among students has been enthusiastic. The program focuses on the industrial sector of the economy. It has not yet expanded into the service sector.

In Pennsylvania, sixteen sites across the state — community colleges and other suitable venues — offer youth apprenticeship programs. By establishing these neutral sites, the program sidesteps many of the complications that often arise from linking multiple schools and workplaces. The apprenticeships offer a solid grounding in a high-tech environment and serve students and employers well. They are not, though, fully integrated into the general school system, something that I believe is critical to maximum success.

Another program began recently in Wisconsin. It builds on an already strong tech-prep curriculum, so it is well on its way to meeting high educational standards. Wisconsin has also overhauled its guidance system and is working on linking high-school work-based learning programs to both two- and four-year state postsecondary institutions. The number of programs and occupations is limited so far, but state support systems for expansion are being put in place.

Arkansas has begun combining postsecondary education with its apprenticeship program. Originally begun by Governor Bill Clinton, an aggressive tech-prep strategy is being adopted throughout the state. Through this network, postsecondary education plays a major role in youth apprenticeships, which by nature determine what level of training students are given. To date, Arkansas has not specified an overall program model.

Project ProTech in Boston, which is discussed in Chapter 5, is perhaps most successful in connecting youth apprenticeship and some of Boston's top employers. The program really helps students to understand how their school education applies to their future. They work in hospitals and other technical facilities, getting a sense of what they must learn to get along in the world of tomorrow. The program offers juniors and seniors twelve to fifteen hours per week of structured work experience, which is connected to their classroom learning. Case managers help support the young people as they go between the worlds of school and work. The students learn they are part of a workplace; they also learn the day-to-day discipline of good performance on the job.

I scrutinized all the programs described above, and though I thought they were, each in their own way, an excellent beginning, none of them combined all the elements that I strongly believe are essential to lasting success.

As I considered a program for Maine and thought about the problem at the national level, I realized that I should draw upon the best aspects of each of these other programs. I also became convinced that any successful apprenticeship program must be firmly grounded in two fundamental principles: first, the plan must offer an educational choice that makes sense to the student; and second, the program must command respect in the community. Without these elements, youth apprenticeship could quickly become a passing fad, and we'd be right back where we started. That would mean losing the opportunity to provide a rewarding education for students who do not plan to go to a four-year college.

Once my design team and I had assessed other programs and discussed Maine's needs, I felt we were ready to go. Our program was crafted by a team with a lot of expertise. It was chaired by President Fitzsimmons, with substantial input from then commissioner of education, Eve Bither; commissioner of labor, Chip Morrison; and my special assistant in the governor's office, Dave Lackey. Several of their deputies, and representatives of the University of Maine, the Maine State Board of Education, and Jobs for Maine's Graduates (JMG), rounded out the team. My own input came from the experience I had garnered in various positions: as chairman of the Education Commission of the States, an organization of all the governors, chief state school officers, other state and local education officials, and key state legislators who have major responsibilities for education; as chairman of JAG, the nation's largest, most consistently applied model of school-to-work transition for at-risk and disadvantaged young people; and, finally, as a member of the Governors' Task Force, which set national educational goals for the year 2000.

Throughout the design process, we never lost sight of the need to involve the larger community. Our team met with leaders of industry, small businesses, vocational education, organized labor, and teachers' unions to make sure that their ideas and concerns were taken into consideration. Our model was ultimately based on a combination of the Danish and German apprenticeship systems and, of course, what was already working in this country. Our aim was to offer students a combination of secondary and postsecondary academic learning that would be broadened by experience at professional work sites. We expected that, with their cooperation, we would be able to integrate employers into the schooling process.

After much consultation, deliberation, and just plain tinkering, we came up with a program I believe can be a model for the country. The nuts and bolts are crucial to our program, and I'll describe them first. But the five general principles we were able to draw from all those nuts and bolts are just as important.

The Maine Youth Apprenticeship Program is a three-year course, which begins after successful completion of the tenth grade. Students participate in comprehensive workplace learning during the eleventh, twelfth, and thirteenth years of schooling. In the ninth and tenth grades, students take part in discussions exploring career choices. We are designing a tenth-grade Gateway Assessment test that all students will take, designed to determine admission into the apprenticeship

MAINE YOUTH APPRENTICESHIP PROGRAM MODEL

GRADE

9	10	11	12	13
Career Exploration	First Semester Regular Academic Program	Apprenticeship First Year	Apprenticeship Second Year	Apprenticeship Third Year
Regular Academic Program	Testing	20 Weeks at High School	20 Weeks at High School	16 Weeks at Technical College
	Focused Career Exploration	30 Weeks Working for Employer	30 Weeks Working for Employer	34 Weeks Working for Employer
	Apprenticeship Selection Testing		Student Receives High-School Diploma	Student Receives One-Year Technical College Certificate and Certificate of Skills Mastery
	Apprenticeship Chosen			

Source: Center for Youth Apprenticeship, Southern Maine Technical College, South Portland, Maine.

program — and also to show that they have mastered the specific skills called for by Maine's Common Core of Learning.

Job specialists from the JMG program help ninth and tenth graders learn about career opportunities so that they can begin to think about their goals. Ultimately, students will be asked to develop individual career plans that outline the steps they will take to reach their goals. They will decide what they hope to attain and then, whether it is a college degree or specific skills training, plot a rigorous path for themselves. (To strengthen this process even more, we are beginning to explore seventh- and eighth-grade career awareness programs for all students, developed by JMG in conjunction with the Maine Occupational Information Coordinating Council [MOICC]. This early career counseling will gradually ease students into this critical process. Such an approach may also demonstrate to these youngsters the practical relevance of an education.)

During the tenth grade, the jobs specialist from JMG begins to identify students who might be candidates for apprenticeship. Working closely with teachers, the specialist helps to steer each student's choice of curriculum and also ensures that those who wish to compete for youth apprenticeships will pass the Gateway Assessment test.

To be eligible for a youth apprenticeship, tenth graders must demonstrate a mastery of specific academic skills and display social maturity and motivation. Of course, the student must also pass the Gateway Assessment test. Based on a variety of factors — including teacher recommendations and past work — the test is specifically geared toward determining the student's proficiency in basic skills. The test not only judges a student's success in finding the correct answers but also the process taken in reaching those answers.

The Gateway

The Gateway Assessment test will complement the successful Maine Education Assessment (MEA), which is a similar, performance-based test administered in the fourth, eighth, and eleventh grades. The MEA provides comparative data that help in assessing school improvement and student success.

The Maine Youth Apprenticeship Program is designed to be an option for eligible students from every high-school program, including college preparatory, tech prep, vocational education, cooperative education, and general education. Students can choose from a variety of occupations, which are limited only by available employment and future job prospects. We have been careful to avoid making it an "alternative education" option for students — and thus eliminate the stigma of "voc kids," who take technical courses because they aren't academically oriented. Students will demonstrate their academic abilities through performance on the Gateway Assessment, ultimately earning a Certificate of Core Mastery, and will be eligible to begin the work-based portion of the apprenticeship in the eleventh grade. Some students may actually enter the program during the preceding summer.

Approximately twenty weeks are spent in academic work at school, and thirty weeks are spent working for an employer, who will provide workplace supervision and teaching.

In the twelfth-grade year, the second year of the apprenticeship, the student's schedule is again divided into twenty weeks of school and thirty weeks of work. After demonstrating satisfactory progress at both work and school, the student receives a high-school diploma at the end of the academic year. The student has now completed high school, but the apprenticeship continues.

It is this third year of apprenticeship — immediately following high-school graduation — that distinguishes Maine's youth apprenticeship from other vocational and cooperative education courses. Our program incorporates a thirteenth year of schooling. During that year, students spend sixteen weeks at one of Maine's technical colleges (shortly to be expanded to include all accredited postsecondary institutions) and thirty-four weeks working for an employer.

Upon satisfactory completion of the final year of the apprenticeship, students receive a one-year certificate from the technical college. This certificate is the equivalent of the first year of an associate degree at the college and can be used to confirm participation in the program, to continue technical education, or for transfer toward a four-year baccalaureate degree. The state is currently working to ensure that the certificate is accepted and offers some degree of credit at colleges and universities outside of Maine.

At the same time, students receive a certificate of skill mastery from the professional, occupational, or industrial group sponsoring the apprenticeship. This certificate lists the skills the apprentice has acquired. We have established, as an important part of our program, that an employer can arrange for additional schooling at no cost for any apprentice who does not measure up to the employer's standard. The student can take any remedial courses necessary to upgrade his or her skills to certificate level.

Maine's program is unique in that it has five distinct parts to it — the five basic principles I mentioned earlier:

1. A new partnership between business, labor, and schools.
2. Systemic change in education.
3. Good liaison between students and support services.
4. Education beyond high school.
5. A guarantee of first-class achievement.

Business-Labor-Education Partnership

This new partnership lets industry and labor work with education to develop the standards new employees must meet, and to determine what will be taught at the work site and what will be taught at school.

The key to a successful program is creating the appropriate focal point to coordinate the effort. In Maine, we decided to establish a Center for Youth Apprenticeship. Its job is to guide the program and coordinate the development of the curriculum. Because Maine's technical college system plays a central role in our program, we decided to house the Center at Southern Maine Technical College in South Portland, Maine.

Although our model is a private entity within the technical colleges, other programs could use a nonprofit corporation, a department or bureau within state government, or any similar college campus arrangement.

The Center for Youth Apprenticeship, although connected to state government, remains autonomous. By setting up the Center within an established technical college, we gave the program needed stature. And by keeping the Center distinct from the state government bureaucracy — and by housing it at a technical college campus — we also made it clear that this program differed from others being directed from the state capitol in Augusta. Schools and colleges look differently on programs that are administered outside the state bureaucracy. In working with businesses, too, the Center's independence is a significant advantage in attracting the necessary youth apprenticeship slots.

Instead of charging the Center solely with the administration of the program, we gave it three further responsibilities: program management, research and curriculum design, and program evaluation. This means managing the nitty-gritty of the program and being responsible for working with our state's Department of Education in many areas of research and curriculum. The Center not only works with the Department of Education to develop the curriculum, standards, and criteria that guide the many different youth apprenticeship options, but after counsulting with other states and communities, it has also recently branched out into "meister" training — we've borrowed the German word and use it to mean a skilled craftsperson acting as a mentor.

The Center is important not only in the coordination of student progress, but also in the development of youth apprenticeships. It must also ensure appropriate quality control. Overseeing Center activities is a Skills Standards Board, chaired by a private-sector representative. This committee was established to make certain that Maine's program would be driven by industry and employer needs, not by the interests of the education community alone. I am convinced that Maine's approach has met with success because we have listened to — and valued — the input of employers and labor representatives. We learned this lesson early on and we haven't forgotten it.

As we considered the youth apprenticeship options that we hoped to provide in our 1992–93 pilot program, we determined that several fields offered the good jobs that Maine's youth deserves. Along with metalworking and insurance, we wanted to create slots in health care. What could be better, we thought, than apprenticeships in the highly sought-after lab tech jobs in our hospitals?

As the program developed, I did my best to keep my finger on its pulse. All seemed to be going well until one day when John Fitzsimmons called with bad news. Earlier in the day, he had met with the human resource directors of the hospitals in the Greater Portland area. They weren't enthusiastic about our program. They felt that they couldn't guarantee jobs for youngsters, even with the necessary skills. Instead, they pointed to the medical records field and said there was a strong demand for those skills.

John and I discussed this development. We had

both been hoping for the lab tech apprenticeship because it was a high-tech job that was attractive to students. But once I got off the phone, I thought a little more and called him back. It occurred to me that we should be pleased, not unhappy — because the system had worked. In fact, the more we thought about it, the more we realized we had just been through a major learning experience. It made clear to us how crucial it was to let the employer set some of the parameters. Instead of training students for jobs that looked great on paper — but for which opportunities didn't exist after high school — we were being shown where the real need for workers was. And that in itself was a significant shift from the way things have been done for generations.

The views of these hospital human resource directors forecast a major change in the way educational programs are run. Historically, educators have decided what courses should be taught — generally without much regard to whether or not employers were interested in the skills students were receiving. The hospital administrators taught us an important lesson — for an apprenticeship to work, it must target areas where employers see a future need. To show that things do work out in the end, we are also designing a more advanced, cross-trained health care apprenticeship that will give students more skills than those of a simple lab technician.

After working with employers to develop the specific youth apprenticeship choices, our Skills Standards Board establishes what we call craft committees. These are made up of representatives of the industries involved: unions (if the occupation is unionized) and educators representing both secondary and postsecondary education. The craft committee determines what's needed for a youngster to become skilled in a specific occupation — and to receive certification for completion of the youth apprenticeship. To date we have established youth apprenticeships in related job "clusters" such as computer support services, office administrative services, customer service, medical rehabilitation therapy, banking and finance, insurance, tool-and-die and metals industries, and electronics and telecommunications. In each of these areas, a targeted craft committee determines the skills that are necessary to complete the program from both an academic and a work-based standpoint.

The craft committee also determines the appropriate curriculum needed to master these skills, which are then cited on the certificate presented to the student upon completion of the youth apprenticeship. These certificates offer portable credentials, which can be shown to businesses in Maine or elsewhere.

In close cooperation with participating employers and others familiar with the occupation, the craft committee also designs a final examination that is administered at or near the completion of the apprenticeship. Students must satisfy rigorous standards before they can graduate from the youth apprenticeship program.

There is more to an employer-driven program than standard setting. For years now, corporate executives have been talking about the need to improve the United States' educational system. Many have called for sweeping reforms that would radically update our schools and guarantee that students graduate as skilled workers. Despite all this rhetoric, the executives themselves have been able to do little more than offer cash contributions to schools, or to provide "job shadowing" opportunities for young people. Youth apprenticeship gives business and industry the chance to put their money where their mouth is. They must now be willing to identify specific youth apprenticeship positions within their own companies.

This often means reevaluating the entire way they do business. And that is for the best.

When we began our Greater Portland pilot program in 1992, many of the participating employers were skeptical. Kevin Healy, a vice president at UNUM, admits that he was not sure how seventeen- and eighteen-year-olds would fit into UNUM's corporate culture. After all, as one manager told me, UNUM is a company that in the past was even reluctant to hire University of Maine graduates because of a perception that their reading levels were frequently low. (Fortunately, that is no longer the case, thanks to the improvements made throughout the university system.) UNUM's human resources department was somewhat concerned about students showing up with "purple hair and cutoff jeans." After all, UNUM is a Fortune 500 company that demands competence and professionalism in all aspects of the business.

Interestingly, students didn't come to work in cutoffs. In fact, just the opposite has happened. The kids have had a wonderful experience and have been model prospective employees. Dottie Schultz, who is meister to one of the students, sums it up best: "We thought the UNUM apprentices were ringers. Now we realize all the apprentices are ringers. We miss them when they're at school — as colleagues, as workers, as people." UNUM has found what others have determined as well: the apprentices quickly adapt to the corporate culture because they see how valuable the learning experience is to their future prospects.

Even during the interviewing process it was clear that those seeking to participate in the program understood the change in lifestyle required. In fact, one of the girls, after a week of interviews and job tours, confided her relief to her guidance counselor: "I'm glad that's over. I've run out of my mother's clothes!"

Jurgen Kok is among those who were skeptical. The vice president and general manager of the Nichols/Portland Division of Parker Hannifin Corporation, he has seen a vanishing work ethic. He told me about the difficulties he has had.

"Punctuality, how to relate to peers, how to dress — these are very basic things. Take coming back from breaks. We expect workers to come back after breaks. We don't watch them, and there's no whistle that tells people to come back. We just laid off a person — fired is a better way to put it — after extending the probation once for ninety days. We had to give a warning, and it still didn't sink in. We did that two more times."

But Kok, who participated in an apprenticeship in Germany himself, views the program as a real opportunity to improve the future for young people. "Youth apprenticeship sets you out on the right foot and stays with you forever. It is important to get the right start. Today the transition from school to productive work life is so difficult. Being a youth apprentice provides a defined path, which takes a load off the minds of the young workers and allows them to look forward to the future with some certainty, at least in their occupational area."

But Kok's experience with youth apprentices is not isolated. Others in the program have watched them shine, and, with their excitement about learning, lift the morale of existing employees. Mickey Greene says that in exploring the best training methods for the youth apprentices, Blue Cross and Blue Shield was forced to reexamine training programs for its own employees. "Youth apprenticeship is not a job training program. It is not a make-work program. It is a program that provides skills for the future . . . for the jobs of the future. There's no downside. It's good for the community, it's good for the business, and it's great for the kids."

As Greene observes, one of the side benefits of youth apprenticeship is that it can lead to a reevaluation of existing company programs and through the process become a learning organization. One of Greene's top deputies, Elizabeth Shorr, senior vice president for corporate relations, has said, "This program has been more work than we ever dreamed it would be, but we would do it again. There have been unexpected benefits in increased worker morale."

Because apprenticeships do require changes in the normal way of doing business, we began our pilot program mainly with large employers. Through their experience, we were able to put together how-to manuals detailing the role of meisters in directing and coaching apprentices at the work site. We have also begun meister training for those who will be working directly with the kids. The manuals make it much easier for smaller businesses to participate because they don't have to "reinvent the wheel."

Unique to Maine is our policy of paying the youth apprentices. They're not considered employees of the firms where they work. Rather, they're classified as employees of the Center for Youth Apprenticeship. As such, they receive a stipend for participating in the program. The funds are generated by a five-thousand-dollar annual fee from participating employers, which amounts to slightly more than minimum-wage earnings for the thirty weeks of work. The twist here is that we pay the students fifty-two weeks a year, regardless of whether they're at the work site or at school. This underscores our conviction that students participating in the program should be rewarded for their effort. Therefore, after the administrative costs — and fringe benefits such as workers' compensation insurance — are taken out, the remainder is distributed to the apprentice in fifty-two weekly installments of about ninety dollars each. The students actually "earn while they learn." As we were designing the program, I recalled that former secretary of education Bill Bennett had said to me that once the program was up and running, our problem would not be attracting enough students, but rather attracting enough slots for students who would want to learn a skill while earning eighty to ninety dollars per week, even if they ultimately planned on going to an Ivy League college. Secretary Bennett's words have since proved prophetic. We have no problem attracting candidates. Our toughest job has been convincing businesses to participate, but we are making progress.

Systemic Change

It has been ten years since the educational reform movement was jump-started by publication of "A Nation at Risk." That study provided a wake-up call for states and educators across the country. In the ensuing ten years, the reform movement in education has become a cause that is perhaps unmatched in U.S. society today. Businesses spend millions of dollars a year to support experimental programs that offer remedies. Schools spend a good deal of time "visioning" and reengineering their curriculum. And governments — especially governors — exert considerable thrust trying to bring about changes in the system. In the process, we have found that there are a number of innovative approaches that show promise. To date, however, no program or group of programs has truly made a difference in the improvement of overall education. We have learned that Americans are very good at trying out new programs but are perhaps not patient enough to see these programs through to full fruition.

Simply tinkering around the edges of our education system, however, is not enough. We need to create incentives in today's society for our schools to change. Our system currently doesn't reward those who take risks in education. Indeed, it is rare to find the principal or superintendent who has experimented with the system — and been promoted. Yet in the business world, innovation and experimentation are often rewarded — which may explain why our businesses are among the most productive and competitive in the world. But in education, most teachers, administrators, and, yes, school board members are not able to imagine, much less experiment, with a new way of teaching.

We are too often restrained by what we perceive as given limits, which stop us from thinking boldly and creatively about change. If we are to reform our schools, we must think along fundamentally new lines. Youth apprenticeship is the place to begin.

A good example of a reluctance to take risks is the "general education" track. Many now refer to this track as "nowhere prep," because most of the young people on this path will not qualify for a college education and aren't prepared for jobs in the workforce, either. Progressive school districts such as the one in Biddeford, Maine, are abolishing the general track courses. By ensuring that all students get the kind of education they need to be productive and contributing citizens, Biddeford has not only increased its scores on the Maine Education Assessment test but also increased the percentage of those going on to college from 43 to 49 percent in the last two years. The school districts in Lewiston and Westbrook, Maine, and in Tulsa, Oklahoma, are also revamping their high schools to be more responsive to students' needs in the new economy.

Flexibility is critical to these programs' success, and that in itself is a dramatic change for schools. For a century, schools have been based on an agrarian school year and been run on a rigid school day. Bells have divided classes. Students have sat through fifty-minute classes, even when a longer class time provides a better teaching and learning environment. School reformers have found out very quickly that trying to change the existing, rigid school schedule is a daunting undertaking indeed.

In youth apprenticeship, however, both the school year and the school day are flexible and, in fact, may vary from site to site and occupation to occupation. By coordinating with employers and focusing on student success instead of arbitrary school schedules, we immediately begin to alter all the accepted conventions of our educational system. During the junior and senior years in high school, youth apprentices — as we mentioned earlier — are in school for about twenty weeks and at work for about thirty weeks; during the third year of the apprenticeship, students spend sixteen weeks in school and thirty-four on the job. We have learned to be responsive to the needs of both businesses and schools in determining how these weeks will be apportioned. Some schools divide the twenty weeks into two ten-week periods, whereas others divide the year into four five-week periods. Still others alternate weeks, and some divide the week itself. "Youth apprenticeship is seen not as a program, but as a process," says Jackie Soychak, principal of South Portland High School. "We must recognize that learning takes place inside and outside the classroom."

This year, we hope to turn the school year upside down as we begin an apprenticeship in tourism. To accommodate the unique needs of Maine's tourism industry, which is at its peak during the summer months but relatively slow during the winter, we may well reverse the current school and work calendars in some of our participating schools. Specifically, we envision the first sixteen weeks of the apprenticeship to be on site to ensure that students receive work-based learning during the busy time of the year for our hotels and restaurants. This change in the calendar would allow students to be back in school from October to May for their academic schooling and remain available for the next summer's surge in the tourist season.

During the pioneer year of our program, for example, students took classes daily from 7:45 A.M. until 2:00 P.M., and worked right through the February school vacation. Students' curriculum included such subjects as workplace safety, team building, and general behavior expected in a job. At the same time, they also studied the traditional subjects of history, math, English, and science. The curricula for these required subjects were developed in conjunction with individual high-school departments, augmented by input from participating businesses.

In order for apprenticeship programs to be flexible, our State Department of Education has had to change from an enforcer of rules to a facilitator of innovation. One good example is our move to a guarantee of quality, which will be described in more detail later in the chapter. Rather than focusing merely on "time served" in school — four years of English and math, two years of a foreign language — we are demanding that students reach certain levels of proficiency and then backing up our effort with a guarantee of quality. It is this guarantee that entitles an employer unsatisfied with an employee's skills to send him or her back for remedial work until the student measures up.

Maine is at the forefront among states in determining an appropriate curriculum and in establishing standards for its students. In 1988, I created the Commission on the Common Core of Learning, which issued its report in 1989. "Maine's Common Core of Learning" is a consensus document, developed by a commission of forty-four citizens from education, business, labor, and government. The document defines the skills and knowledge that students need to succeed in the world of tomorrow. Instead of setting forth graduation requirements, the commission established benchmarks for every student and gives us the opportunity to build those benchmarks into the school curriculum.

A second commission is currently developing Maine's "learning results," which will be the standards that help determine levels of knowledge. In Maine, we provide schools with a great deal of autonomy in applying the common core. Our state has no mandated curriculum, nor do we mandate learning tools such as textbooks. The latitude we give schools in applying the common core is an excellent demonstration of the strategy that makes youth apprenticeship such an attractive and acceptable approach to educational reform.

Most of the skills and most of the knowledge that we expect of students at high-school graduation can be taught in the workplace as well as in the classroom — and often with greater impact. Students rapidly learn responsibility and citizenship — and can more easily grasp the relevance of their education once they are in the workplace. "I used to think I was a stupid kid," one apprentice told her guidance counselor at West-brook High School after three months in the program. "Now, I know I'm not."

Matt Burr, an apprentice from Gorham who works at D&G Machine Tools, told me, "I never saw the need for English, because I planned to work with my hands. My meister has made me see the importance of English, no matter what I plan to do." Midway into his apprenticeship, Matt is throwing in precalculus, physics, and advanced English.

We have also found that we can combine work- and school-based curricula so that students can receive credit for the work they are doing away from school.

Youth apprenticeship provides for change in the system by allowing students to "earn while they learn." As I have mentioned, in our system, employers pay our Center for Youth Apprenticeship five thousand dollars annually for each youth they accept. The earn-while-you-learn concept not only serves as an incentive for students to work hard both at the work site and at school, but it also eliminates the need for students to find dead-end part-time jobs. It gives them a chance to concentrate their energies on learning.

Education after High School

A program of youth apprenticeships must include, at the very least, one year of college as part of a student's preparation. The key to the wide acceptance of our program is the third year. That is the time when students are offered postsecondary courses, and it is valuable for two reasons: first, it enhances the prestige of their career choice; and second, it instills in many students a taste for lifelong learning.

As is discussed in Chapter 2, the world of work has changed radically, giving rise to the need for all of our students to have some college-level education. Though such college-level courses will not replace traditional baccalaureate degrees, they will offer yet another important pathway to success.

One of the most misunderstood aspects of the future workforce is the kind of skills that will be required. Contrary to popular belief, only 30 percent of all jobs in the early years of the twenty-first century will require four-year college degrees. Yet, 85 percent of available jobs will require some kind of post-high-school technical training. A four-year college degree is, obviously, not the only avenue to an improved standard of living anymore.

For youth apprenticeship to overcome the general reaction that "this is fine for someone else's child, but not good enough for mine" response, there must be a college component to the program.

When Harry Truman introduced the GI Bill after World War II, he probably didn't realize the effect his action would have on education. We have since spent fifty years promoting the idea that college leads to success in life. Indeed, our entire educational system defines success as matriculation at college. The alternative of training for a good career, and forgoing college, is often ignored. Since we have spent fifty years urging people to go to college if they want to be a success, I do not believe that the general public will ever support the idea of promoting any educational pathway that does not include at least some form of college learning. Our apprenticeship program does that, and only in doing so will we find the support we need to expand youth apprenticeship in the United States.

Our program's third-year postsecondary experience gives students just such opportunities. Though, at its inception, only our technical colleges are participating, we are expanding in 1996 to a number of our university campuses as well.

We have structured the program so that all youth apprenticeships lead to one year of college — halfway to an associate degree. We also have agreements with our colleges that credits — and students — can transfer automatically, so they can continue their education beyond an apprenticeship if they so desire. For example, the University of Southern Maine and Southern Maine Technical College have already agreed that the university will accept all students who have completed the apprenticeship program successfully at the technical college. We also hope to involve Maine's private colleges in the program.

Through craft committees (discussed earlier in this chapter) we are able to design appropriate standards and curricula at the colleges. It is important to remember that the purpose of the program is to make certain that its graduates possess the skills employers are looking for. A close working relationship between businesses and colleges ensures that students not only pass their exams at the end of the three-year program but are also prepared for the world of work.

Ultimately, the federally funded tech-prep program and youth apprenticeship program will be quite similar. The major difference will be the greater stress on applied academic learning in the former, whereas the latter will emphasize work-based learning. Students in either program, if they follow through, will be eligible for an associate's degree. In addition, students in the youth apprenticeship program will receive a certificate from the industry or occupational group that oversees their particular apprenticeship that they have mastered the skills established by the industry. Thus, over time, I believe that apprenticeship will be increasingly demanded by students who want to ensure that they not only have academic skills, but also workplace skills.

As our system develops, I believe it will also create competition for students among our colleges. The eight hundred dollars the colleges will receive for their participation in the third year of the apprenticeship will, in many instances, cover the incremental costs. In other instances, the apprenticeship slots could serve as "loss leaders" for the college to attract students who will then stay on for two- or four-year degrees. Whatever the result, the system will mean more choices for students.

Youth apprenticeship has also dramatically changed the focus of college education. For the first time, Maine's technical colleges have guaranteed admission to students in the apprenticeship program. This is a tremendous shift, and an expression of faith in the youth apprenticeship program overall.

Student Services Liaison

Beginning a new job is challenging for all of us, and especially for young people who are unsure of their skills. A successful youth apprenticeship model will assign student services liaisons to help students adjust to the workplace, and also to keep the student connected with academic study. Whenever new programs are created, you can expect growing pains. These challenges can be all the more dramatic when a program requires the coordination of several participants — and this is especially so in education. In youth apprenticeship, we must balance the needs of three groups: school, business, and student. To minimize any growing pains and maximize positive results, the Maine program drew from the experience of centuries. In European youth apprenticeship systems, students participate in "youth guilds" that give a real sense of belonging and provide needed interaction with other students. To instill a sense of responsibility in all involved in the program, we ask each of the three participants to sign an agreement specifying certain responsibilities. Businesses, for example, must guarantee that their apprentices are actually learning the appropriate skills. Schools need to adapt their curriculum and perhaps rearrange school schedules to meet the apprentices' academic needs. For students, this contract means showing up and behaving appropriately. Needless to say, such a complex three-party agreement needs a mediator or facilitator.

Students especially need a coach or advocate, not just during the preliminary discussions of their obligations but throughout their time in school and during the transition to the workforce. In order to be able to provide liaison services for students, their employers, and the schools, we have chosen to modify the JAG school-to-work transition program implemented by

JMG in Maine. Many of the skills JAG teaches, in both its twelfth-grade school-to-work transition and Opportunities Awareness dropout prevention programs, are skills that benefit student apprentices. Specifically, students receive training in self-esteem, appropriate interview skills, résumé writing, community service, social skills, workplace relationships, and career preparation. In addition, each of the states in the JAG network has a career association, which is much like other student organizations, such as 4-H clubs and Vocational Industrial Clubs of America (VICA). Students meet periodically, raise money for their local and statewide meetings, and engage in community service activities.

But aside from this extraordinary "standard" work, job specialists also go the extra mile for the students. Melissa Morel Milne, a JMG job specialist in Biddeford, told me about her first problem case: a young man who had lost his motivation for school and work. "It was my first home visit, and I was a little nervous," she explained. "I took a deep breath and rang the doorbell. Behind the closed door, a dog barked, and I wondered if phone counseling would be enough for this young man. But when he opened the door, I knew Tim needed more. He told me his dog didn't bite. I walked inside, shook his hand, and looked him in the eye — but maybe I should have looked down first. Tim was wearing Kermit the Frog slippers, and at first I thought he might have some kind of psychological problem.

"*The Price Is Right* was on, and an afghan was draped over his shoulders. He was the epitome of a lounge lizard. I talked with him over the television, and then invited him over to his kitchen table. I took out the classified sections from three newspapers and asked him to highlight anything that caught his eye. He was so lethargic, acting as if this was a grueling task, and I knew what he wanted. He wanted me to give up and leave him alone.

"I realized," Melissa continued, "that Tim needed me to be firm, but not overwhelming. His mother had passed away a few years ago, and he took it hard. Tim really needed some extra attention and motivation. I gave him a power talk, and a week and a half to find a job. Today, Tim is leading a productive, happy life with a full-time job at Rufus Deering Lumber in Portland. He still needs consistent follow-up. But the system works."

Not every student needs the kind of attention that Melissa gave Tim — but when students need help, our student services liaisons can provide support — and sometimes a little guidance and encouragement are all it takes. JMG provides liaisons for each of the schools participating in our program. Students interested in apprenticeships participate in ninth- and tenth-grade career exploration programs run by JMG staff. Those ultimately selected continue to work with JMG liaisons — writing résumés, interviewing, and finally selecting the appropriate apprenticeship. The liaison stays with his or her students throughout the three-year apprenticeship and for the first nine months after completion to help them make the transition from school to full-time work or college.

Because we worry about teenagers being taken out of the everyday life of their schools, we have also adapted the JAG career associations to our program.

We call these student support teams "student guilds." Like German guilds or JAG career associations, the youth apprenticeship guild elects officers, does community service, and serves as a focal point for those students who are in the program. This kind of interaction among students helps them share common experiences and gain the self-confidence they need to succeed in the program and beyond.

Jobs for America's Graduates has a broad range of experience in working with young people who, by dint of their schooling, home lives, financial situation, or other factors, are "at risk." We intend to make use of this experience in Maine's program by using JMG job specialists to help prepare those youngsters who perform poorly on our eighth-grade Maine Education Assessment tests and need additional help in order to pass our tenth-grade Gateway Assessment. This two-year remedial program will serve to increase the number of youngsters who can qualify for apprenticeships. Remedial attention will also be given to those who do not do well on the tenth-grade test but who still want to prepare for the apprenticeship program. Our program does not simply target kids who are at risk. Sometimes even the finest students have trouble in school and need more real-world relevance in their studies. One guidance counselor told me, "This program is the best thing that has happened to Sally. Apprenticeship and after-school track are the only things keeping her in school." Another principal told me, "I am excited about this program. It's perfect for this student — because we were going to lose him."

We will continue to assist all students who need to

upgrade their skills in order to qualify for an apprenticeship. Our purpose is not to exclude students but rather to provide them with an incentive to increase their skills so that they qualify for the program.

Quality Guarantee

In Maine, we guarantee the quality of the education and the skills possessed by participating students. The certificate from the Maine Youth Apprenticeship Program is proof of a student's competence. Needless to say, if we are to maintain high quality, students must understand the basics of education before beginning the youth apprenticeship.

Our guarantee is simple: if a student does not possess the skills we have certified, then our technical colleges (or appropriate high schools) will retrain them free of charge. We have a wonderful example of customer satisfaction in retailer L. L. Bean. Not surprisingly, Bean is also a major participant in our youth apprenticeship program. Their customer satisfaction guarantee is the same sort of satisfaction we guarantee employers of those youngsters who complete the youth apprenticeship training.

I recall a rule proclaimed by another of our participants, the Osram Sylvania subsidiary of Siemens Corporation. The company's two rules of quality are:

1. The customer is always right.
2. If the customer isn't right, see rule #1.

If we are going to transform our educational system into one that brings accountability and respect to its product — the students — then it needs to be more customer-driven. Employers need to treat schools like suppliers and provide the input and support necessary to ensure that they are receiving a quality product — our young people. That may sound a little bald and bare when speaking of people and their lives, but it happens to be the truth.

This is the approach that many of our employers have taken. At UNUM, Kevin Healy says his company views their participation as a tool to ensure both well-skilled workers and better schools. "This is a long-term investment because it is costly to make a bad hire. We are already getting our money's worth — because our youth apprentices are contributors to the team."

Employers can avoid the cost of turnover, training, and hiring of new employees by participating in local schools and taking part in screening and training. Don Wescott, project coordinator for Nichols/Portland, says that his company sees the youth apprenticeship participation as a tool for improving its workforce as well. "At Nichols, we're seeing a radical change in the skills needed by our workers. We would like to focus on advanced training; up to now, we have had to focus on basic skills training. We believe the apprenticeship program will change that." The minimal cost to a participating employer is a good investment compared to the hit-or-miss nature of hiring new employees. By combining a three-year apprenticeship with our insistence on quality, we will develop both a better qualified workforce and lower the costs of hiring. More will be acquired for less.

Through the rest of the 1990s and on into the

twenty-first century, economic competition will be won by the societies that are the best educated — where people at every level have received the most farsighted and gain-producing preparation. It is the education of those who do not go to college that now matters most, for it is they who make the real difference today in a society's productivity. And it is precisely that essential segment of U.S. population that has been neglected in our schools. Youth apprenticeship is the answer to that problem.

If it worked in Maine, why shouldn't it work elsewhere? Our state is the easternmost in the nation — the new day breaks here first.

8

*Getting Started:
Designing a Youth
Apprenticeship Program
in Your Community*

THERE'S AN OLD MAINE STORY about a tourist asking directions to L.L. Bean from a sea captain who's sitting on his front porch in Freeport. He tells the out-of-stater to take a right at the church, go two blocks, take a right at the service station, then go three blocks, and take a right by the market. Ten minutes later the traveler shows up back at the sea captain's home and says, hopping mad, "I'm right where I started. What's going on?" To which the captain replies, "I had to see if you could take directions before I gave them to you."

Now that you've read this far, and listened to some basic directions, I hope you have been moved to start a youth apprenticeship program in your own community. Remember, this will not be an easy task to undertake; but it will be ultimately worthwhile. You will need diplomacy and patience, and there will be many letters to write and meetings to attend before you can expect to see positive results.

As governor, I was the motivating force behind the youth apprenticeship program in Maine. In spite of my strong personal interest in the development of the program and the support of a design team led by the president of the Maine Technical College System and my senior staff, it was one full year before any students in Maine were enrolled in work-based learning with business employers. Even though the program began with only a modest fifteen students, many experts around the country found it hard to believe that we were able to organize and establish youth apprentice-ships in such a short time — even with the governor leading the effort.

Don't expect instant success, and don't allow your-self to get discouraged. There will be plenty of people who will explain to you why such a program cannot work. Your reply should be, "It has to." You should remember, however, that it will take at the very least one year to organize the effort and another to design the youth apprenticeship program that is appropriate for your area. To be successful you must keep telling yourself that if you believe, as I do, that our educational system is not producing the well-trained students that U.S. industry urgently needs, this is your chance to help.

Whenever I talk with people around the country who are interested in establishing a youth apprentice-ship program in their state, I remind them of the words of the Irish statesman and orator, Edmund Burke. "No one," he said, "made a greater mistake than he who did nothing because he could do only a little." You can avoid that mistake and in the process make a huge difference in the future of this country by joining our revolution to change the way we prepare our youngsters for work.

The rest of this chapter will tell you how you can get started and how you can assemble a task force to prepare for and design a youth apprenticeship program. It will also tell what the individual members of your task force can do in their own spheres of influence and areas of expertise to make the program a reality. Also, Appendix A and Appendix B give two examples of state laws on youth apprenticeship. Appendix A is a JFF-proposed model state law. Appendix B is the law we passed in Maine.

How to Begin

There is an old saying that a journey of a thousand miles begins with the first step. The effort to institute change in any system always faces uncertainty concerning the first steps to be taken and who will take them. You can take those first steps, which I hope will set you on the journey toward creating a brighter future for youngsters in your community or state.

First, you should find out about and get in touch with existing school-to-work programs in your state or in your region. Try to visit one of them. There is no substitute for seeing firsthand how school-to-work partnerships operate. Talk to participating employers, workers, teachers, and students, and find out how these programs really work.

You may also want to reread Chapter 7 on the

Maine program to familiarize yourself thoroughly with its contents and remind yourself how a youth apprenticeship program differs from other school-to-work alternatives.

If you feel that you would like still more information, you will find a list of organizations at the end of this chapter that can answer your questions and supply you with further details.

Once you are knowledgeable about youth apprenticeships, you can approach your local business community, your schools — teachers as well as administrators — local labor unions, and, of course, the students and their parents. Suggest to them that you form a task force to explore the possibilities of putting together similar programs in your schools. You will probably find that many of the people you approach will need to be educated before they understand what a youth apprenticeship program can do to help young people get good jobs and supply business with the skilled workers needed for the future.

What a Task Force Can Do

All the members of the task force should participate in the planning right from the start, and everyone's voice should be heard in all significant decisions. It is important to emphasize at the opening meeting that it will take at least two years for the apprenticeship program to become operational. And don't forget that it is vital that all participants understand and agree on their roles; otherwise, misunderstandings are bound to arise.

For that reason alone, a representative membership in the task force is crucial. A local or regional effort should have members from the following groups:

- The local chamber of commerce.
- Other local business organizations.
- School administrators and teachers.
- Local colleges.
- Unions.
- Parents and parent organizations.
- Students and student organizations.

If you are organizing a state task force, you should add representatives of the state's departments of education, labor, and economic development, as well as representatives of vocational education and the state's higher education council.

1. Your task force should get in touch with the national headquarters of the various local groups you are in partnership with. For business and industry contact the U.S. Chamber of Commerce, the National Association of Manufacturers, and the Business Roundtable. Labor unions can also be helpful, and don't overlook the teachers unions. A variety of government associations such as the National Governors Association and the National Conference of State Legislatures can give you guidance. Parent-teacher organizations willingly share information with their membership and appreciate information from you about your efforts. You might also want to contact Jobs for the Future, Jobs for America's Graduates, or the Center for Youth Apprenticeship in Maine.

2. A visit to Europe can be very encouraging. More than 60 percent of German and Danish youth take part in apprenticeship programs. Seeing such programs operating successfully on a large scale can be an eye-opener, and talking to European (and U.S. multinational) employers about their participation will confirm the value of such programs. Several organizations can help you organize, and sometimes pay for, a trip to Europe for this purpose.

Center for Learning and Competitiveness
University of Maryland at College Park
College Park, MD 20742
(301) 405-6330

CDS International, Inc.
330 Seventh Ave.
New York, NY 10001
(212) 760-1400

German Marshall Fund of the United States
11 Dupont Circle, NW, Suite 750
Washington, D.C. 20036
(202) 745-3950

3. If it is not mainly composed of state officials, your task force will find it helpful to write a letter to your governor and your state representatives, and to directors of agencies that deal with employment or education. You can get their names and addresses from your local public library or from the office of your state representative.

In the letter you should explain that you are interested in creating a youth apprenticeship program. Ask if you can work with your state government agencies in their efforts to establish such a program in your community and in your state. Appendix C is a letter which may serve as a model. Adapt it any way you want to, so that it reflects your particular situation and concerns.

4. There are programs and incentives operating at the state and national levels that can either help or hinder your local activities.

On the plus side, states and the federal government can provide funding. They also distribute guidelines for the curriculum, how to assess progress, how to develop a staff, and how to establish credentials. The help you get from these national and state institutions can save you from reinventing the wheel.

On the minus side, you may find that the profusion of federal and state education and/or economic programs overlap, creating a bureaucratic tangle that can make it hard to reach the people who can really help. Persistence is the only answer here.

At the state level, the following institutions and organizations may be participating in school-to-work and youth apprenticeship planning efforts:

- Governor's office.
- State legislature.
- Department of Education.
- Institutions of higher education.
- Department of Labor.
- Department of Economic Development.
- Business councils and industry associations.
- Labor organizations.

You should also examine state initiatives on educational reform. They will include employment counseling, worker retraining, industrial modernization, human resource councils, college funding incentives, and anything else that will affect developments in the workforce and the labor market.

5. At the federal level, there are several initiatives that may help:

- The School-to-Work Opportunities Act of 1994 awards federal grants to states developing school-to-work programs, with the majority of funds going directly to local programs. In addition, the legislation sets up a clearinghouse for information on pioneering efforts that can then be used by fledgling programs. Contact the U.S. Department of Education or U.S. Department of Labor for information.
- The federal government has already funded more than a dozen nationwide associations to develop industry-recognized standards for occupational skills. Another new law is called Goals 2000: Educate America. This law establishes a National Skills Standards Board to work with industry in setting voluntary standards for occupational skills. To find out more about this legislation get in touch with the U.S. Department of Education, U.S. Department of Labor, or an industry association.

Also, Anne Heald, at the Center for Learning and Competitiveness at the University of Maryland can be helpful.

6. To design an appropriate youth apprenticeship program, it is important that you look at the future

labor needs of your local area. Here are some questions you should ask:

- Where do the companies find their workers now?
- What is the projected demand for employees in the coming years?
- Is the local workforce aging? Where will new workers come from?
- Is the customer base of these companies becoming more diverse? If so, how can we diversify our workforce to serve this new customer base?
- Where can a company hire skilled workers who are well trained and understand industry needs?
- Are there clear pathways for career growth within a company or an industry?

7. Finally, you should set up a design team to develop the program. As I discussed in Chapter 7, we have found that it makes sense to have both secondary and postsecondary curriculum experts on the team, as well as representatives from business associations who have experience in training. Sometimes the human resource directors of major corporations can be of great help.

The design team should consider these areas:

- How to administer and finance the program.
- How to design the content of the program.
- How skills and standards can be evaluated and tested.
- How the curriculum can be developed and coordinated.

- How to set up student support systems.
- How to recruit people to run the program (both in the school and at the work site).

Jobs for the Future has produced a "tool kit" for design teams based on lessons from innovative programs around the country. For additional information that would be helpful to any new program, contact JFF at the address at the end of this chapter.

How Others Can Support Your Efforts

The Business Community

The greatest barrier to full implementation of youth apprenticeship programs across the country is, in my view, a surprising lack of understanding within the business community of the importance of the apprenticeship movement.

Therefore, it is critically important to find business people in the community to urge local companies to participate. Without employers, there can be no youth apprenticeships.

1. Here are ways that members of the business community can involve their workplaces in the program:

- See if they can find examples of similar organizations that are involved in apprenticeships.
- Talk to their human resources departments or personnel directors about ways of engaging students in work that complements their schooling.
- Find out from employees if they would be in-

terested in becoming mentors, or meisters, to young people. Many workers in existing programs find that teaching a young person about their job rekindles their own enthusiasm for it.

2. Employers can help students on a work site by setting up the following system:

- Designate one employee to manage the work site, and give that person visible support from above.
- Make sure that union or worker representatives are included in planning sessions from the beginning.
- Make absolutely certain that workers know that they will not be displaced by student trainees.
- Train and reward staff for their teaching and coaching roles.
- Make sure that payment methods (for example, piecework) are adjusted so that workers who serve as trainers are not penalized.
- Have top management make it clear that the program has a high priority, and ask them to show their support by sponsoring students in their departments, by explaining both the executive function and the industry's overall picture, or by serving as meisters themselves.

3. Business today must change processes continually to keep up with competitors and customer demand, so narrow job training isn't good enough anymore. Employers need employees who understand how their

jobs fit into their industry as a whole and who can adapt to new demands.

To achieve such diversity in a youth apprenticeship program, business should take the following steps:

- Rotate students through job shadowing or internships in different departments early in their training, so that they can get an idea of the company as a whole and also decide on a specific field for later, in-depth learning.
- Pair students with work site meisters who have broad organizational responsibilities and can introduce their charges to the entire industry.
- Choose work-site trainers and meisters who can be good role models. Look for someone who gets along well with people and enjoys teaching and coaching. These skills are just as valuable as technical expertise.
- Give students increasingly complex assignments that develop planning, organizing, analyzing, and problem-solving abilities.

Educators

Teachers and administrators can have a significant influence on the way the apprenticeship concept is received in schools. The best way to avoid suspicion, resentments, and misunderstanding in schools is to include teachers, guidance counselors, and administrators in all the planning discussions. Discussion should focus on finding areas of common interest among employers, workers, parents, and educators. Most should agree that one of the fundamental goals is to produce motivated students who value learning because they see its relevance to the working world. For a program to succeed, it must have the support of the vast majority of the school staff.

Youth apprenticeship programs run two risks in academic circles. On one hand, some educators may be afraid that a program incorporating work-based learning won't have enough academic rigor — that it will be a curriculum for the "dumb" students. On the other hand, there are other educators who may see such a program, with its team of teachers, its administration, and its employer support, as a privileged program and therefore resent it. By explaining the whole concept in detail to the school staff, you can get their cooperation before going ahead.

1. To have a successful program, school administrators must be willing to:

- Attend a school-to-work summer institute. (Jobs for the Future sponsors such an annual event.) This is an invaluable opportunity to learn from other people's experience. Bring along a program learning team, including teachers and counselors. Together, they can help build a common vision of the program's potential.
- Set aside joint planning time for teachers, counselors, and industry partners, to facilitate interdisciplinary learning. The strongest links between school and work are forged in programs that focus on a student's academic instruction as

it applies to the issues and the themes encountered at work. For school and work to reinforce each other, not only *what* is taught but *how* it is taught must change. In interdisciplinary learning, students are taught by teams of teachers; they are exposed to a range of subjects drawn from both academic and vocational sources, but all centered on a common theme. Teachers are no longer lecturers. They become partners with the students in an approach that integrates the practical with the theoretical.

2. To facilitate this new approach to learning, schools can:

- Schedule youth apprenticeship students and their teachers to meet together for core academic classes.
- Utilize team teaching by combining industry representatives and teachers from a variety of disciplines.
- Make sure that teachers, counselors, and industry representatives meet often for joint sessions to coordinate school lessons.
- Introduce a system of student assessments that measures how well students are able to link ideas and how well they can relate academic concepts to vocational goals.
- Provide joint staff and curriculum goals.
- Set aside specific times for students to assess their work experience. This can be done in class or in career counseling sessions.

3. Measuring a student's progress is absolutely es-

sential for the success of such a departure from traditional ways of teaching. Here are some methods that others have initiated:

- Have students answer the following questions about their work experience: What is the primary purpose of the organization where you are working? What are the responsibilities of your department? What are your personal responsibilities? How does your job relate to the overall organization? Who do you work most closely with? Are computers used on the job? If so, in what capacity? What types of math applications do you see at work? (These are just sample questions — the more inventive and specific your questions are, the better.)
- Have students keep a journal in which they write about the world of work and their place in it. Use journal entries as starting points for classroom discussions and career exploration sessions.
- Create project assignments that draw on students' work experience and their skills in academic subjects from math to English.
- Have students explain their work to an assembly of school- and work-based personnel.
- The curriculum can teach students the larger aspects of their jobs. They can acquire an understanding of planning, management, and finance, of technical and production skills, of the underlying principles of technology, of labor and

community issues, and of the issues of health, safety, and the environment.

4. Support services are necessary to attract students to a youth apprenticeship program. Unfortunately, most guidance counselors focus almost exclusively on four-year college choices and know little about the local labor market. In Maine, we have addressed this problem by making use of the resources and expertise of Jobs for Maine's Graduates. We have developed a guidance system that helps students who are not college-bound by supporting the activities of JMG and of the Maine Occupational Information Coordinating Committee. Here's what schools can do:

- Make sure that students start thinking about career possibilities in junior high school. This can include field trips and occasional release time from school to allow students to observe, and perhaps participate in, the work of their parents or of a neighbor.
- Develop a program of supervised job shadowing for seventh- through tenth-grade students that gives them direct, hands-on experience with employers. Work out a series of steps, built on the practical knowledge gained through job shadowing, which will prepare a student for a specific career.
- Make sure that a student gets good guidance in the choice of possible careers.
- Contact the national offices of JAG (address at the end of this chapter) for more ideas on how

to ensure that students get all the information they will need to make the choice that is right for them.

Local Colleges

As I have emphasized throughout this book, postsecondary involvement in a youth apprenticeship program is critical to its ultimate acceptance in this country. The program must include at least one year of college, and the credits for the program must be at least partially transferable toward a two-year or four-year college degree.

1. Representatives of local colleges can involve the local college community in support of your efforts in the following ways:

- Encourage colleges to work with employers on modernization projects as well as on research development ideas.
- Help colleges develop courses based on occupational themes.
- Arrange for admission credits for youth apprenticeship experience.
- Provide for advance placement credits for students who have completed approved courses.
- Suggest to colleges that they begin to incorporate some work-based learning in their technical programs.
- Encourage professors to familiarize themselves with work-based learning through personal contact with the business community.

2. Within the college community, college personnel can advocate postsecondary involvement in youth apprenticeship by using the following national experiences as examples:

- Youth apprenticeship programs around the country have found that some students labeled as not college-bound have actually been motivated, by seeing practical applications of their schooling, to finish college.
- Technical jobs in the future will require the same levels of cognitive skills as those needed in college now. In addition, they will require a level of technical training beyond that which is taught in high schools.
- On a very practical level, focus groups indicate that parents generally do not want their children to participate in programs that entirely exclude college.

Unions

When people first began exploring youth apprenticeship strategies, there was some opposition from segments of organized labor — particularly those connected with the established registered-apprenticeship programs in the trade industries. Times have changed, though, and many in organized labor have become vocal and active supporters.

The following section is written explicitly for union members who want to promote youth apprenticeship. However, most of the suggestions are just as applicable to workers who are not unionized as to those who belong to a union.

1. In May 1993, the Executive Council of the AFL-CIO adopted a statement called "AFL-CIO Guidelines on Skill Training and School-to-Work Transition in the 1990s and Beyond." This statement emphasizes organized labor's support for school-to-work transition programs and specifies concerns, which include:

- The need for high academic standards.
- The importance of involving labor in design and governance.
- The need for industry-created skill standards for both youth- and adult-training programs.
- Guarantees that youth will not displace existing workers.

2. All local labor leaders and activists should be made aware of this statement. For more information on the AFL-CIO's views and activities in this area, contact:

> Department of Education, AFL-CIO
> 815 16th Street NW
> Washington, D.C. 20006
> (202) 637-5000

3. Many unions are involved in efforts to establish school-to-work programs. Each year, new programs are created that have union involvement in their design and administration. If a union is interested in participating in youth apprenticeship, it will be helpful to know about the unions in your state that are already involved. Information is available about others who have started down this road, by contacting:

- The union's international headquarters (most of which are in Washington, D.C.).

- The state AFL-CIO office.
- The Human Resources Development Institute, which is the training arm of the AFL-CIO:

> HRDI, AFL-CIO
> 815 16th Street NW, Room 405
> Washington, D.C. 20006
> (202) 638-3912

Or you can get in touch with:

> Jobs for the Future
> 1 Bowdoin Square
> Boston, MA 02114
> (617) 742-5995

4. Bringing young people into the workplace often, understandably, makes the existing workers anxious about their jobs and their futures. These fears and misunderstandings can be avoided if the unions sit down with management early in the design process to discuss how workers' concerns can be addressed. Current employees and the unions that represent them want to make certain that bringing young people into the workplace will not result in layoffs or loss of work. Indeed, it would be a shortsighted public program that put young people in part-time jobs at the expense of adult wage earners.

Here, briefly, are some ways in which workers can protect their jobs:

- Have the program construct a basic agreement that protects existing workers from displacement. The School-to-Work Opportunities Act includes such safeguards and can serve as a model. The Act prohibits the displacement of any currently employed worker or a reduction in nonovertime work, wages, or employment benefits. It also ensures the integrity of existing contracts and collective bargaining agreements, as well as the applicability of health, safety, and civil rights laws.

• Make sure all parties understand that training and mentoring students in the workplace takes working time from adults that could otherwise be used toward production. Make sure payment methods (such as piecework) are adjusted so that workers are not penalized.

5. In the United States today, about three hundred thousand individuals are enrolled in joint labor-management apprenticeship programs, primarily in the building and construction trades. The organizations that administer and support this system — known as the registered apprenticeship system because its programs are registered with federal or state labor departments — should be actively enlisted in discussions of school-to-work initiatives.

As Paul Cole, secretary-treasurer of the New York State AFL-CIO puts it: "The key is for advocates of school-to-work transition efforts to support — and not interfere with — existing registered apprenticeship programs in return for knowledge and guidance about how to develop their own systems, incorporating high standards, portable credentials, curriculum and assessment strategies, recruitment and selection procedures, teacher training, and other key components of long-established registered programs." At the same time, Cole emphasizes, the registered apprenticeship system and its advocates must work not only to ensure protection of their own programs but to encourage the development of new ones in other industries. Job creation benefits everyone.

Parents

Parents can contribute a great deal to the success of youth apprenticeship programs. They can sponsor opportunities for students in their own workplaces and encourage others to do the same.

Parents shouldn't think that youth apprenticeship programs are designed exclusively for the non-college-bound student. Focus group research shows that a parent's major fear is that such programs will provide narrow job training and will preclude their children from going to college. Yet experience with pioneering programs indicates quite the opposite; many students previously seen as non-college-bound discover that they enjoy learning, that they can succeed beyond expectations, and that to get a good job they need more than a high-school diploma. In addition, cognitive science research shows that even academically successful students improve when they see the practical results of their studies.

1. Parents can make it their duty not to let the program become a "second-class" learning option. They can work with the school board, school improvement councils, and other parties to:

- Make sure the program isn't training students for a single job, such as "lathe operator," but rather for a broad range of occupations in a particular industry, such as manufacturing, health care, printing, or financial services.
- Insist on rigorous academic content.
- Insist on a range of postsecondary school options, including two- and four-year college and advanced training programs.
- Make sure postsecondary educational representatives are included in the planning process.
- Schedule a discussion of school-to-work programs at parent-teacher meetings. Talk about how these programs are designed to motivate academic learning by making it relevant to future jobs.
- Arrange a discussion with successful local companies to talk about the skills workers need.
- Explore the fears and desires of parents regarding their children's participation.
- Choose a representative of their organization to participate in the planning process.

2. The more parents learn about career choices, the more they can share this knowledge with their children. They can contact the local chamber of commerce for information about companies in their area. Find out if companies will allow parents to visit them with their children or with a school group. Or they can also:

- Contact the local community college and see if they can visit its career counseling and placement office.

- Set aside an occasional Saturday as an "exploration day" at the local library with their children; ask the reference librarian for appropriate sources of information on career choices.

3. Check out the guidance department at the local high school:

- Does it have information on local employers, occupations, and projected job openings, or is it simply focused on college entrance?
- Does each student go through a goal-setting process whereby he or she identifies a range of post-high-school goals and learns what is needed to achieve them?
- Make sure that career guidance is an integral part of the curriculum.

4. They can talk to the management at places where young people currently work. They can also:

- Work with local stores and restaurants to expose students to the management, accounting, and marketing functions of their operations.
- Ask that existing summer job programs be converted to year-round apprenticeships.
- Start a community effort to get current employers to require good grades as a condition of employment, or at least to review their student employees' report cards with them.

5. A parent can also talk to local youth and community organizations and request that they include career counseling among their activities.

- Some organizations, such as Junior Achievement, already include a work readiness section.
- Other organizations, including scouts, boys and girls clubs, and the YMCA, could easily include visits to local businesses, talks by local employers, and other work preparation activities.
- Local community groups can introduce young people to their own finances and management.
- Sports clubs can take a behind-the-scenes look at professional sports and find out what is needed to get jobs in the field.

The purpose of this book was to identify the problems bedeviling our economy, and then — with JFF's help — to offer solutions. But there was another purpose as well: to inspire the reader to take action, to make a difference. One way or another, the problems created by the new world of work affect us all, and it will take the efforts of all of us to convert those problems into opportunities seized and mastered.

These are some organizations you can contact for further information:

Jobs for the Future
1 Bowdoin Square
Boston, MA 02114
(617) 742-5995

Center for Youth Apprenticeship
Southern Maine Technical College
Fort Road
South Portland, ME 04106
(207) 767-5210

Council of Chief State School Officers
One Massachusetts Ave. NW, Suite 700
Washington, D.C. 20001-1431
(202) 408-5505

Jobs for America's Graduates
1729 King St., Suite 200
Alexandria, VA 22314
(703) 684-9479

National Alliance of Business
1201 New York Ave. NW, Suite 700
Washington, D.C. 20005
(202) 289-2917

National Center for Research in Vocational Education
University of California
2150 Shattuck Ave., Suite 1250
Berkeley, CA 94704
(800) 762-4093

Southern Regional Education Board
State Vocational Education Consortium
592 Tenth St. NW
Atlanta, GA 30318
(404) 875-9211

U.S. Department of Labor
Office of Work-Based Learning
200 Constitution Ave. NW
Room N4649
Washington, D.C. 20210
(202) 219-5281

U.S. Department of Education
Office of Vocational and Adult Education
400 Maryland Ave. SW
MES Room 4090
Washington, D.C. 20202-7100
(202) 205-5451

Epilogue: Why It All Matters

PEOPLE OFTEN ask me why all this matters — whether a youth apprenticeship program is really necessary to meet our nation's needs. "Our schools weren't so different when *I* was a kid," someone will say. "Why change something that worked so well for me?"

The answer, of course, is that the times are different, very different. The fact is that our country is changing — and not always changing for the better.

The wage gap between the educated and the uneducated is growing — to a point that makes society as we know it unsustainable.

Rather than just accepting change as something we can do nothing about (except putting more police on the streets and building more prisons), we must examine the root causes of the changes we are seeing.

I believe that the cause can be found, generally, in the lack of jobs that pay a decent, living wage. And why is that?

The reason, to me, is clear. We cannot hope to compete successfully in the global marketplace without sophisticated technology that enhances productivity. To operate that technology, however, requires workers with the most developed skills. But too few of our workers or graduating high-school students have those skills. The Commission on the Skills of the American Workplace gave its report the apt title "High Skills or Low Wages." I believe that those are indeed our stark options as we approach the twenty-first century; we face a choice between jobs that demand high skills for high salaries or low-skill jobs whose pay falls far below the standards to which Americans have grown accustomed.

Those who care about the future of our country ask how and where we are going to find a remedy. I am convinced that we need to reform both the U.S. school and workplace.

During the Industrial Revolution, productivity grew by a factor of about one hundred from 1850 to 1950. Since the microprocessor revolution took off in the early 1970s, productivity in some areas has increased by a factor of more than one million.

Many of our larger businesses have already begun the painful process of catching up with this latest revolution. They have invested billions of dollars in new technology and in intensive training of their employees. These improvements caused their productivity to increase, and today U.S. business leads the world. Our improvements have far outpaced gains in Japan or Germany.

As I discussed in Chapter 5, though, there are warning signs that we should watch. In recent years, the annual growth in productivity has been cut in half. From the end of World War II up to the 1970s, the annual growth rate ran about 2.5 percent. Since then — throughout the 1980s until the early 1990s — growth shrank to 1 percent or less each year. At the same time, the gap in productivity between this country and its competitors also diminished; it is now less than 10 percent higher than Canada, Norway, and Sweden; less than 20 percent higher than Japan, Germany, or France.

The good news, however, is that productivity trends in America have improved.

U.S. business has learned over the past few years that to improve productivity, it must readjust three fundamental business structures: the production process (making it possible for workers to produce more per hour), investment in technology (the production of better products in the same amount of time), and the education and retraining of workers — which alone can account for about a quarter of all growth in productivity in a given year.

Although businesses know where to target their investments, most of them have not resulted in new jobs. Instead, our new surge in productivity has resulted in *fewer* new jobs, accompanied by a greater demand for higher skills, both in the new jobs available and in existing jobs.

This reality creates the great paradox of the productivity gains made in America over the last few years — these gains have not been accompanied by a corresponding increase in our standard of living. This phenomenon is caused by the inadequate skill level of American workers, who are often rendered obsolete by technology. Once workers are laid off, they begin looking for new work. The good jobs, however, require the very skills which they do not have.

In order for our standard of living to increase it is necessary that we address in the short term the need for increased skills among our unemployed. For the long term, we have to ensure that students coming out of our schools have a strong work foundation upon which they can build. A youth apprenticeship system begins to take them down that road.

There is no doubt now that U.S. business is staying competitive — but at the expense of the unskilled American worker. A survey of middle-sized businesses conducted by Grant Thornton in 1990 found that more than two thirds of the companies interviewed felt that they had a problem with productivity. Yet more than half of these companies looked upon the problem as a minor one, probably because they believed they could solve it simply by replacing their workers with new machinery.

Today, much more than a basic skill like reading is needed. There are few jobs for those who do not know algebra, and fewer jobs still for those who lack basic problem-solving and teamwork skills. No, the days of the unskilled worker in a high-wage job are finished.

Yet despite these harsh realities, our schools have frequently dragged their feet about change. Though our schools do recognize that the best students need a better education, they still overlook the "forgotten half" of the student body, those children who don't plan to continue their education toward a four-year college degree. Yet it is just these children who need our schools to teach them more and better skills if they are to be equipped for today's job market. Left to fend for themselves, as they so often are today, they constitute the greatest threat to our future standard of living. Youth apprenticeship can change all that.

We can only be successful, however, if we also address the equally urgent necessity to change the way U.S. businesses operate — especially the kind of small and midsized companies that are predominant in my state. They must adjust to modern technology and to the demand for a highly competitive workforce.

Not surprisingly, there have been myriad reports and studies that have examined our changing times and the implications they bring in their wake. From the news media to individual corporations, from state governments to the federal government, all eyes have been focused on ways to improve the modern workplace.

One such study, "The Secretary's Commission on Achieving Necessary Skills," was ordered by the U.S. Department of Labor. The final report, issued in 1992, found five "essential" requirements for good job performance today:

1. *Resources:* A student must be able to identify, organize, plan, and allocate resources, such as time, money, material, facilities, and human resources.
2. *Interpersonal:* A potential employee works well with

others; understands the demands of teamwork, teaching, customer service, leadership, and negotiation; and knows how to handle change and diversity.

3. *Information:* A student must be able to use computers to process information and to evaluate, organize, interpret, and communicate the information he or she has acquired.

4. *Systems:* The student must understand, monitor, and know how to improve or design systems.

5. *Technology:* A student must be able to select and apply appropriate technology, and maintain and troubleshoot equipment.

A *Fortune* magazine survey, published in June 1993, identified trends affecting businesses, especially those that are becoming more productive by downsizing. According to *Fortune:* The average company will become smaller and employ fewer people; traditional hierarchical organizations will give way to a variety of organizational forms, especially networks of specialists; technicians — from computer repairers to radiation therapists — will replace the manufacturing workforce; horizontal divisions of labor will replace vertical divisions; the pattern of doing business will shift from making a product to providing a service; and last, work itself will be redefined to encourage and even require constant learning. The old nine-to-five mentality will be replaced by a higher order of thinking.

There will be, ultimately, a shift in the approach of business to better and better quality in its products. Continual improvements and customer satisfaction will be valued more highly than mass production by rote. During 1991 and 1992, I served on Secretary of Labor Lynn Martin's National Advisory Commission on Work-Based Learning. The commission came to these same conclusions about business trends and our economic future.

During my tenure on the commission, I realized that many of our larger companies were already modernizing their work sites and their workforces. The pace of that modernization has only increased since then. Other businesses, however, are taking what, I believe, is a shortsighted step. To lower their costs, they are simply moving operations to third world countries. I am convinced that this action is ultimately self-destructive. If enough companies follow suit, we will gravely undermine the United States' standard of living. Instead of enjoying the fruits of a productive, technological revolution — as we once enjoyed the fruits of the Industrial Revolution — we could instead experience ever-increasing crime and an ever-widening disparity of income, leading to civil disobedience and social unrest. We cannot allow this to be America's future. We must, rather, adopt policies that allow businesses to be competitive and hire American workers. This will not be easy.

It is achievable, though. One of the leading advocates of apprenticeship programs around the world is the president and CEO, managing board, of Siemens AG in Germany, Dr. Heinrich von Pierer. The ability of American workers to respond to the apprenticeship concept is obvious from Dr. von Pierer's words:

Siemens does not believe in apprenticeship merely for its educational value. We believe in it because it makes a bottom-line difference. We have practiced apprenticeship for over 100 years and, in our collective judgment, it gives our company a worldwide competitive edge. Today we have apprenticeship programs in sixteen countries. Among those are three different models established in the United States for testing.

Some have suggested that American workers do not meet the standards of workers elsewhere in the world. This is not so. In fact, the first-year apprentices at our test site at Lake Mary had collectively the highest test scores after the first year of any of our apprentices anywhere in the world!

The American workforce will clearly benefit from a major investment in apprenticeship. The "raw material" in America has proved second to none when properly trained and prepared. This is why we are aggressive investors in America and in the American workforce.

For small businesses, meeting the challenge of modernization is a daunting prospect. They lack the facilities, expertise, and resources to upgrade their workforce. Therefore, if the system does not change, they too will contribute to our worsening economic climate.

The work-based learning commission found out, very quickly, that the key to achieving first-rate skills and good wages does not lie with worker training and education as separate pursuits. Rather, learning should be based on the integration of school and workplace, so that future workers can use their knowledge and training to solve problems and also be stimulated to continue the learning process. It is a revealing statistic that, over the past fifty years, fully 60 percent of the growth in workplace productivity can be traced to work-based learning.

Japan and Germany are two countries, among others, that have invested heavily in work-based education. We must do the same if we are to compete in world markets. To build a well-trained labor force, we, too, must invest in education, both in schools and at U.S. work sites.

Throughout the pages of this book, I have tried to build a case for the importance of forging a new dynamic relationship between school and business. Without it, youth apprenticeship programs cannot hope to succeed.

During my lifetime, schools have remained isolated from business. Historically, teachers have done their job to educate students; business has then taken the graduates and taught them what they needed to know to do their jobs. As a result, a school staff member still does not truly understand the needs of business, nor does the business community truly know how youngsters are taught in our schools.

Youth apprenticeship creates a direct connection between workplace and education. I am convinced that this is an important first step toward building a link between one community and the other and developing a new U.S. system for improving the skills of our labor force.

A dynamic relationship between business and schools will ensure that one can learn from the other. U.S. business can establish standards for the skills they need to be competitive, and schools will be able to upgrade their capacity to meet these high standards. Educators will be able to develop appropriate curricula while business can keep them informed on its changing needs.

As educators and the business community continue to work together, the standards demanded of students will become clearer and clearer. With such standards, it will ultimately become possible — sometimes as early as the tenth grade — to certify students according to their mastery of their studies. Then, when a student graduates, his or her diploma will truly mean something, spelling out the range of skills possessed by the student.

A youth apprenticeship system will also influence and improve the in-house training of existing workers. As meisters teach apprentices, coworkers will recognize the importance of improving their own skills. That, in turn, will easily lead to a dialogue between schools and businesses on the best ways to meet the training needs of existing workers.

The result of the dialogue will be a realization that the structure established to support a youth apprenticeship system can easily be modified to establish a work-based learning program for existing employees. And that will set in motion a series of new partnerships designed to integrate training of future workers while upgrading the skills of those already in the workforce.

I do not believe that this country is prepared to spend the billions of dollars necessary to create a completely new — and expensive — infrastructure to train employees now working in small and middle-sized companies. But a youth apprenticeship system can put in place the necessary facilities, expertise, and resources that businesses need to design a process of lifelong learning and skills enhancement for all of their employees.

Students in a youth apprenticeship system spend about half their time at a work site; during that time, schools are left with a partially unused physical plant that could be used for classes to upgrade the capabilities of existing employees. And when youth apprentices return to the classroom, those employees can return to their jobs with new skills. Such a venture between businesses and schools can produce a synergy that supports youth apprenticeships and also meets the needs of businesses to improve the current workforce.

Maine's youth apprenticeship program has already shown how this process can work. Jurgen Kok of Nichols/Portland is the chairperson of Maine's Skills Standards Board. He told me that his company's participation in the program has inspired some of his workers to develop their skills further.

"Our employees have always seen overtime as the only way to make more money. I have always told them that if they were to spend the same amount of time enhancing their skills — and we pay tuition up

front — then their paychecks would *always* be bigger."
Since his company began its participation in youth apprenticeship, more and more workers have chosen additional training. "Because of its focus on education and training, we believe this program will promote lifelong training for our current workers as well as for our apprentices," Kok said.

As this reciprocal system develops, and our schools and businesses integrate complementary programs, we will build a true, lifelong learning system. Schools will work in concert with employers, and the worlds of practical work and education will be linked, giving our children, as well as our current workforce, a training that is both academic and work-based.

That accomplished, I believe we will credit a new youth apprenticeship system with having helped America turn the corner, bringing with it increased productivity, reinvigorated schools, and, especially, renewed prosperity.

Appendix A.
Model State Law*

A BILL TO BE ENTITLED

"THE (STATE) YOUTH APPRENTICESHIP ACT"

BE IT ENACTED BY THE LEGISLATURE OF THE STATE OF _____:

SECTION 1. SHORT TITLE.

This Act may be cited as the "_____ Youth Apprenticeship Act."

SECTION 2. DEFINITIONS.

In this Act:

(1) "Articulation" means a formal agreement between a secondary and a postsecondary educational institution that defines a

*This is the model for a youth apprenticeship program proposed by Jobs for the Future.

continuous course sequence for a youth apprenticeship learning program and specifies all requirements for advanced standing in the postsecondary institution and transcripted credit for postsecondary learning completed by youth apprentices during high school.

(2) "Assessment" means the formal process by which a youth apprentice demonstrates mastery of academic and occupational competencies in order to meet educational objectives and industry skill standards expected of a youth apprenticeship learning program.

(3) "Gateway assessment" means a performance-based assessment that determines whether a student is able to read, write, compute, and perform in mathematics, physical and natural sciences, technology, history, geography, politics, economics, and English at the tenth grade level.

(4) "Integrated learning" means the process that connects academic instruction with occupational education, work-based learning, and work experience.

(5) "Occupational credential" means a certificate that is awarded to a youth apprentice as the result of a satisfactory assessment.

(6) "Registered apprenticeship" means the apprenticeship program that is governed by Sec. 333, _____ Education Code.

(7) "School-to-work transition" means the process by which a student who has a demonstrated mastery of basic academic skills, as represented by satisfactory performance on a gateway assessment, acquires practical and technical knowledge to progress into a productive and satisfying job or career in the labor force.

(8) "Structured work-based learning" means the portion of a

youth apprenticeship program that uses the workplace as a learning environment and consists of a planned sequence of job assignments, worksite instruction, and formal on-the-job training.

(9) "Youth apprentice" means a student who is at least 16 years of age and is engaged in a structured program of integrated learning as specified in a youth apprentice agreement.

SECTION 3. YOUTH APPRENTICESHIP SYSTEM.

(a) The department of education, with the cooperation of the department of labor, the department of technical education and community colleges, the board of regents, and the department of commerce, economic development, and job training, shall establish a comprehensive system of youth apprenticeships to prepare high school students for high-skilled professional and technical employment. The system shall provide for youth apprenticeship learning programs within each school district that offer high school students a range of occupational choices and enhance a student's prospects for productive employment, continued education, and career development. The department shall give priority to developing youth apprenticeship learning programs for technical occupations that offer entry-level jobs with good opportunities for advancement into high-skill, high-wage careers.

(b) A youth apprenticeship learning program means a program that has a specific industry or occupational focus, combines secondary and postsecondary academic instruction with structured work-based learning, and leads to the award of a high school diploma, a postsecondary credential, an occupational credential, or advanced placement in a registered apprenticeship. A youth apprenticeship learning program must involve, at a minimum:

(1) organized career development for all students, beginning with career awareness in elementary school and in-

cluding career exploration and community service activities beginning no later than eighth grade and continuing through the high school years;

(2) entry by any high school student, beginning in the 11th or 12th grade, who has demonstrated mastery of basic skills through satisfactory performance on a gateway assessment and has completed an educational portfolio that includes classroom products;

(3) an organized program of integrated learning that includes high standards of academic instruction, structured work-based learning, and year-round work experience;

(4) academic instruction in social studies, humanities, the arts, advanced science and mathematics, and language arts, presented in a manner that helps a student apprentice develop high skills in reading, writing, reasoning, information retrieval, problem-solving, listening, speaking, critical thinking, and working effectively both alone and in a group;

(5) structured work-based learning that is organized to help a student apprentice master appropriate industry or occupational skill standards;

(6) at least one year of secondary education;

(7) at least one year of postsecondary education at a technical college, community college, or institution of higher learning or advanced standing in a registered apprenticeship program;

(8) the payment of wages on a scale that recognizes the progressive acquisition of knowledge and skills by a student apprentice during the term of the program and considers the prevailing wages and compensation for full-time

workers within the occupational area that is the subject of the learning program;

(9) regular performance feedback as well as a satisfactory assessment;

(10) a clear description of all additional requirements, if any, that are necessary for a youth apprentice to qualify for the award of a two-year or four-year postsecondary degree from the state system of higher education; and

(11) sponsorship by a local youth apprenticeship council as defined in Section 5 of this Act.

(c) The department shall provide technical assistance to secondary and postsecondary schools, employers, and local youth apprenticeship councils related to the design and operation of youth apprenticeship programs. Such assistance may include:

(1) curriculum development and integration;

(2) structured work-based learning for youth apprentices;

(3) assessment;

(4) in-service training and professional development of counseling and guidance staff;

(5) in-service training and professional development of teachers and instructors in both schools and the workplace;

(6) articulation agreements;

(7) industry skill standards;

(8) the role of youth apprenticeships in the context of all available school-to-work transition options;

(9) recruitment and marketing of employers and students;

(10) connecting youth apprenticeship and school-to-work transition programs with ongoing reforms of elementary and secondary education; and

(11) connecting youth apprenticeship and school-to-work programs with the system of adult job training and work-force investment.

(d) The department may enter into intergovernmental agreements with any other executive agency to assist in the provision of technical services as described in subsection (c) of this section.

SECTION 4. INDUSTRY AND OCCUPATIONAL SKILL STANDARDS.

(a) The youth apprenticeship policy board shall appoint and convene committees to recommend industry and occupational skill standards for youth apprenticeship learning programs. Each committee shall include, as appropriate, representatives of employer, statewide or national trade associations, workers or labor organizations, and educators who are familiar with the skills, knowledge, and competencies required by exemplary workers in targeted occupations.

(b) In developing and recommending standards, committees shall consider:

(1) key qualifications that are common to all occupations;

(2) skill needs of current jobs in the targeted occupation;

(3) the future skill needs of jobs in the targeted occupation based on reasonable forecasts of technological and occupational change;

(4) skills needed in related occupations;

(5) advanced skills needed in occupations that are related to the target occupations through reasonably indentifiable career ladders;

(6) skill standards promulgated by national trade and industry associations, federal agencies, other states;

(7) standards that would help student apprentices understand all aspects of the industry that is the focus of the standard, including planning, management, finances, technical and production skills, underlying principles of technology, labor issues, and health and safety; and

(8) skills standards that exist for comparable education systems in other developed nations.

(c) The board shall cooperate with the department of education, the department of labor and job training, and the department of technical education and community colleges to ensure that industry skill standards developed for youth apprenticeship learning programs are in accord with skill standards that exist or may be developed for adult workers in job training and advanced skill mastery programs.

(d) The department of education shall make available professional staff to assist all committees in researching, developing, and recommending skill standards.

(e) The board shall periodically review approved skill standards to determine the need for revisions or the adoption of new standards. Every standard once approved shall be reviewed at least once every five years. The board shall establish procedures for incorporating revised standards into existing youth apprenticeship agreements.

SECTION 5. LOCAL YOUTH APPRENTICESHIP COUNCILS.

(a) The department of education, upon the recommendation of the youth apprenticeship policy board, may recognize a local youth apprenticeship council to facilitate the design and operation of youth apprenticeship learning programs within a defined region of the state.

(b) A local youth apprenticeship council must reasonably represent interested groups within its region, and be comprised of employers, industry or trade associations, chambers of commerce, workers or organized labor, parents, community organizations or associations, and employees, administrators, or board members of secondary or postsecondary institutions.

(c) A local youth apprenticeship council may:

(1) approve youth apprenticeship learning programs within its region of operation;

(2) work with secondary and postsecondary education institutions, employers, labor organizations, and other groups, to facilitate the design and operation of all youth apprenticeship learning programs within its region of operation;

(3) facilitate articulation agreements necessary for the efficient operation of youth apprenticeship learning programs;

(4) conduct marketing efforts to recruit additional employers and schools for participation in a youth apprenticeship learning program, including special efforts to recruit minority and female students into apprenticeships involving nontraditional occupations;

(5) provide technical assistance to participating schools and employers;

(6) provide advice and recommendations to governmental units, school boards, local boards of technical colleges, chambers of commerce, and other entities regarding the operation of youth apprenticeship learning programs;

(7) monitor the progress of youth apprenticeship learning programs in meeting program objectives;

(8) collaborate with local youth apprenticeship councils in other regions of the state to jointly develop curricula, provide professional development for teachers and worksite instructors, and share information and experiences about program design and implementation;

(9) if it is incorporated as a not-for-profit corporation under Section 553, _____ Business Code, administer public and private grants and other funds to assist the design, implementation, or operation of youth apprenticeship learning programs; and

(10) facilitate the resolution of disagreements arising in connection with youth apprenticeship agreements.

(d) An entity wishing to be recognized as a local youth apprenticeship council shall submit a written request to the youth apprenticeship policy board. An application must identify the proposed composition of the local council, terms of membership, geographic coverage, organizational form, and other information required by the board to make a decision on the application.

(e) A local youth apprenticeship council shall sponsor all youth apprenticeship learning programs that operate within its region of operation. Each program must meet all the requirements established in Section 3(b) of this Act. The terms and conditions of each youth apprenticeship learning program must be clearly set forth in a written agreement between the employer, youth apprentice, parent of a youth apprentice, and local education agency that describes:

(1) the occupation or occupational area that is the focus of the youth apprenticeship;

(2) specific occupational competencies contained within the industry skill standard applicable to the youth apprenticeship learning program;

(3) all rights and obligations of a youth apprentice, secondary or postsecondary institution, and employer or group of employers with respect to a youth apprenticeship learning program;

(4) the compensation and benefits that will be paid a youth apprentice during the apprenticeship period; and

(5) the secondary, postsecondary, and occupational credentials that will be awarded for successful completion of program requirements.

SECTION 6. YOUTH APPRENTICESHIP POLICY BOARD.

(a) The youth apprenticeship policy board is composed of twelve members appointed by the governor with the advice and consent of the senate. Four members of the board shall represent private employers or employer associations, three members shall represent workers, organized labor, or community-based organizations, three members shall represent local education institutions, and two members shall represent the general public. Appointments should reflect the geographic, cultural, ethnic, and gender-based diversity of the state.

(b) In addition to members appointed by the governor, the board shall include the following ex officio members:

(1) the governor or designee, who shall be a nonvoting member,

(2) the superintendent of public schools;

(3) the commissioner of the department of labor;

(4) the director of the department of technical education and community colleges;

(5) the executive director of the board of regents; and

(6) the director of the department of commerce, economic development, and job training.

(c) Appointed members of the board serve staggered terms of four years with the terms of one-third of the members expiring on February 1 of each odd-numbered year.

(d) Appointed board members shall serve without compensation, but shall be entitled to reimbursement for reasonable and necessary expenses incurred in carrying out required duties.

(e) The board shall:

(1) advise the department of education concerning the planning and implementation of a youth apprenticeship system;

(2) approve industry or occupational skill standards that are recommended by skill committees, and monitor the need for periodic revision or amendments to existing skill standards;

(3) collect and maintain participation and other data on, monitor, and evaluate local youth apprenticeship programs;

(4) ensure that the implementation of the youth apprenticeship system is consistent with state education, labor, or job training standards and policies;

(5) make recommendations to the department of education regarding the approval of entities wishing to be recognized as a local youth apprenticeship council; and

(6) submit a report to the legislature before the end of the 30th day of each regular session evaluating the performance of the youth apprenticeship system and making recommendations for system improvements.

(f) The governor, with approval of the speaker of the house and the president of the senate, may designate an existing statewide public board, council, or commission that has statutory responsibility related to education, workforce preparation, job training, or human investment policy to carry out the duties and powers of the youth apprenticeship policy board upon the affirmative finding that such transfer would further the efficient administration of government.

SECTION 7. SPECIAL PROVISIONS.

(a) All state and federal laws relating to the safety, health, and well-being of workers apply to youth apprentices.

(b) The employment of a youth apprentice may not displace or cause any reduction in the hours of non-overtime work, wages, or employment benefits of any currently employed worker.

(c) The department of labor shall collect labor market information that will assist in the identification of industries and occupational clusters that are characterized by high growth, upward mobility, high wages, and strong technical skills, and are focused on high performance, diversity, and investment in skill development.

(d) The chancellor of the board of regents shall develop and implement a plan for the preparation, certification, and recertification of teachers and workplace instructors who are proficient in developing curricula for and teaching in integrated learning programs.

(e) A portion of state aid to school districts, technical colleges, and community colleges shall be used to fund the costs of planning and operating local youth apprenticeship learning programs. The portion shall be estimated by dividing the total amount of state aid received by a school district or community college district by the average daily attendance of all students enrolled in that district and multiplying the result by the number of youth apprentices who are employed within the district. The department of education may enact rules and procedures for determining the actual amounts of state funds used for youth apprenticeship learning programs, so long as the actual amounts reasonably carry out the intent of this subsection.

(f) The department of education, with the approval of the youth apprenticeship policy board, may enter into an agreement with any private not-for-profit or quasi-governmental organization that has statewide jurisdiction to administer assessments to determine if a youth apprentice has mastered the academic and occupational competencies necessary for the award of an occupational credential. An agreement entered into under this subsection may not exceed a period of three years, and may permit the organization to establish a reasonable fee for its assessment services.

(g) The department of education shall ensure that a student's decision to enter a youth apprenticeship agreement will not affect his or her status with regard to fulfilling all prerequisites for graduation from high school and eligibility to enroll in any postsecondary degree program in the state.

(h) The chancellor of the board of regents shall develop and implement a plan that provides for the award of credit or advanced standing in two-year or four-year postsecondary degree programs for graduates of youth apprenticeship learning programs. The plan shall be submitted to the governor and to the youth apprenticeship policy board no later than two years following the effective date of this Act.

SECTION 8. INITIAL APPOINTEES.

In appointing the initial members of the youth apprenticeship policy board, the governor shall appoint four persons to terms expiring February 1, 1997; four to terms expiring February 1, 1998; and four to terms expiring February 1, 1999.

SECTION 9. EFFECTIVE DATE.

This act takes effect September 1, 1993. Section 8 of this Act applies to tax years beginning on or after January 1, 1994.

Appendix B.
State of Maine Legislation

STATE OF MAINE

An Act to Establish the Maine Youth Apprenticeship Program

Be it enacted by the People of the State of Maine as follows:
Sec. 1. 20-A MRSA c. 432 is enacted to read:

CHAPTER 432

MAINE YOUTH APPRENTICESHIP PROGRAM

ADMINISTRATION AND PURPOSE

The Maine Technical College System in cooperation with the Department of Education and the Department of Labor is authorized to provide comprehensive administrative and financial services to the Maine Youth Apprenticeship Program, a nonprofit corporation organized under the laws of the State of Maine to provide an additional education option, through a partnership between business and education, for high school students and young adults to obtain classroom instruction and on-the-job training that prepares them directly for career-related employment or continued education. The sole purpose of the Maine Youth Apprenticeship Program, referred to in this chapter as "the Program," is to assist the Maine Technical College System, public secondary schools and other publicly supported educational institutions in the State in providing a combination of academic learning and structured work-based learning at businesses in the State to students enrolled at Maine Technical College System facilities, public secondary schools or other publicly supported educational institutions.

The Maine Technical College System is authorized to receive and administer on behalf of the program any grants, fees, charges, appropriations and other funds from whatever source.

GOALS

The goals of the program as delineated by its articles of incorporation and bylaws are:

1. Education and training. To provide a sequential education and training program that enhances opportunities for youth in this State to become highly skilled and productive members of the work force;

2. Skilled work force. To provide a skilled and educated work force for businesses in the State to increase their competitiveness in the global economy; and

3. Economic future. To enhance the economic future of the State and improve its productivity and competitive position in a world economy by creating a skilled and educated work force.

ACTIVITIES

The Program shall provide a sequence of combined school and workplace education and training that has a specific industrial or occupational focus. Students participate in the program for up to 3 years and, while doing so, must be enrolled in a State technical college or other publicly supported secondary or post-secondary school. The program shall offer a curriculum based on industry skill standards recommended by the Skill Standards Board. Participants who demonstrate that they have met these skill standards are entitled to a certificate of skill mastery that describes the competencies achieved by the students.

The Program shall encourage career exploration, applied academic and occupational coursework, paid work and education experience, outcome-based assessment, structured work-based learning and enrollment in a postsecondary educational institution.

SKILL STANDARDS BOARD

1. Establishment. The Skill Standards Board, established in Title 5, section 12004-G, subsection 26-A and referred to in this section as "the board," shall advise the director of the program on the industry skill standards associated with an industry or occupational group that must be mastered in order for a student to be awarded a certificate of skill mastery.

2. Membership. The board consists of 14 members as follows:

A. Three members representing business and industry;

B. Three members representing organized labor;

C. Three members representing education;

D. Two student members who participate in the program;

E. Two members from businesses that participate in the program; and

F. One member representing the State Apprenticeship and Training Council.

3. Appointments. The Governor, the President of the Senate and the Speaker of the House of Representatives shall each appoint one member representing business and industry, one member representing organized labor and one member representing education. The Governor shall appoint 2 members from businesses that participate in the program, 2 student members who participate in the program from persons nominated by the director of the program and one member representing the State Apprenticeship and Training Council from persons nominated by that council.

4. Officers and staff. The officers of the board consist of a chair and vice-chair, elected by the and from the board membership for a term of one year. Officers may be elected for one additional term. The vice-chair serves as the chair in the absence of the chair. The board is staffed by the Maine Youth Apprenticeship Program staff.

5. Compensation. Members are entitled to compensation for expenses, from program funds, according to Title 5, Chapter 379.

Appendix C.
Sample Task Force Letter

Dear _____:

We have recently established a task force to institute a youth apprenticeship program in our [community, county].

I am writing to find out how I can learn about the state's efforts to improve the transition from school to work for our young people. As a [parent, employer, teacher, college president, etc.], I am particularly concerned about finding practical options for students. Our task force believes that youth apprenticeship is the answer.

As you probably know, three fourths of the United States' young people don't finish college before starting work. Eighty percent of students trained in vocational programs never spend one day in the job for which they have been trained. Something is clearly wrong.

Technology has created a global economy. Today, we need to prepare all of our students, not just the 20 percent who receive college degrees, for success in a complex labor market.

Other states, the federal government, employers, educators, workers, parents, and students across the country are working together to establish local partnerships whose aim is to introduce youth apprenticeship programs.

The purpose of these programs is to integrate school learning with supervised on-the-job training, so that each reinforces the other.

Yet another aim is to integrate high-school studies with post-secondary learning (including two- and four-year institutions). Because most of the jobs in the future will require advanced training, integrating the high standards and rigorous content of academic learning with the applied methods of vocational education can give a student a high-school education combining higher education credits and industry-recognized certification of occupational skills.

Specifically, our task force would like to know what plans our state has to create a youth apprenticeship program. How does it plan to make sure that such a program fits into the state's educational and economic development strategies?

I would like to find out who at the state level is working on this vital issue, and how I and our task force can be of help.

I look forward to hearing from you and I hope we will soon be working together to implement this important project.

Sincerely,

Selected Bibliography and Suggested Readings

America's Choice: High Skills or Low Wages. Report of the Commission on the Skills of the American Workforce. Rochester, N.Y.: National Center on Education and the Economy, 1990.

Apprenticeship. Washington, D.C.: U.S. Department of Labor, Employment and Training Administration, Bureau of Apprenticeship and Training, 1992.

Thomas Bailey and Donna Merrit. *The School-to-Work Transition and Youth Apprenticeship: Lessons from the U.S. Experience.* New York, N.Y.: Manpower Demonstration Research Corporation, 1993.

Building a Quality Workforce: A Joint Initiative of the U.S. Department of Labor, U.S. Department of Education, and U.S. Department of Commerce. Washington, D.C.: U.S. Department of Labor, 1988.

Campus Partners in Learning/Campus Compact. *Resource Manual for Campus-Based Youth Mentoring Programs.* Rhode Island: Campus Partners in Learning/Campus Compact, 1990.

A. P. Carnevale, L. J. Gainer, and A. S. Meltzer. *Workplace*

Basics: The Essential Skills Employers Want. San Francisco: Jossey-Bass, 1990.

Council of Chief State School Officers and American Youth Policy Forum. *Building a System to Connect School and Employment.* Washington, D.C.: American Youth Policy Forum, 1994.

Willard A. Daggett. "Future Workplace Is Shocking." *North Carolina Education,* November/December 1990.

Bob Filipczak. "Apprenticeships from High School to High Skills." *Training,* April 1992, pp. 23–29.

The Forgotten Half: Pathways to Success for America's Youth and Young Families. Washington, D.C.: The William T. Grant Foundation Commission, 1988.

From High School to High-Skilled Health Careers: New Models of Work-and-Learning in Health Care. Cambridge, Mass.: Jobs for the Future, 1992.

Mary Agnes Hamilton and Stephen F. Hamilton. *Toward a Youth Apprenticeship System.* Ithaca, N.Y.: Cornell University Media Services, 1993.

Stephen F. Hamilton. *Apprenticeship for Adulthood: Preparing Youth for the Future.* New York: Free Press, 1990.

Stephen F. Hamilton and M. A. Hamilton. "Mentoring Programs: Promise and Paradox." *Phi Delta Kappan,* March 1992.

Michael Hammer and James Champy. *Reengineering the Corporation: A Manifesto for Business Revolution.* New York: HarperCollins, 1993.

Harvard Education Letter. Special Issue on Apprenticeship, vol. IX, no. 2. Cambridge, Mass.: Harvard University Graduate School of Education, 1993.

Investing in Youth: A Compilation of Recommended Policies and Practices. National Conference Sponsored by the National Governors Association. Washington, D.C.: National Governors Association, 1992.

James Kadamus, *The School to Work Connection.* Washington, D.C.: A Report on the Proceedings of The Quality Connection, Linking Education and Work, a national confer-

ence sponsored jointly by the Secretary of Labor and the
Secretary of Education, May 15–17, 1990.

Richard Kazis. *Improving the Transition from School to Work in the
United States*. Washington, D.C.: American Youth Policy
Forum, Competitiveness Policy Council and Jobs for the
Future, 1993.

————. "Two-Year Colleges: What Role Will They Play in
Improving the School-to-Work Transition?" Paper prepared for the American Association of Community Colleges Tech Prep Roundtable. Cambridge, Mass.: Jobs for
the Future, 1993.

Edwin Kiester, Jr. "Germany Prepares Kids for Good Jobs; We
Were Preparing Ours for Wendy's." *Smithsonian,* March
1993, pp. 44–55.

William H. Kolberg and Foster C. Smith. *Rebuilding America's
Workforce: Business Strategies to Close the Competitive Gap*.
Homewood, Il.: Business 1 Irwin, 1992.

Jonathan Kozol. *Savage Inequalities: Children in America's Schools*.
New York: Crown, 1991.

*Learning that Works. A Guide to Youth Apprenticeship Policy and
Practice. Building a Statewide Youth Apprenticeship System:
Conference Briefing Book*. Cambridge, Mass.: Jobs for the
Future, 1993.

Bernard J. McMullan and P. Snyder. *Allies in Education: Schools
and Businesses Working Together for At-Risk Youth*. Philadel-
phia: Public/Private Ventures, 1989.

John Naisbitt. *Megatrends*. New York: Warner, 1982.

William E. Nothdurft. *Schoolworks: Reinventing Public Schools to
Create the Workforce of the Future*. Washington, D.C.: German Marshall Fund of the United States, 1989.

William E. Nothdurft and Jobs for the Future. *Youth Apprenticeship, American Style: A Strategy for Expanding School and
Career Opportunities*. Cambridge, Mass.: Jobs for the Future, 1991.

Paul Osterman and M. Iannozzi. "Youth Apprenticeships and
School-to-Work Transition: Current Knowledge and Leg-
islative Strategy." *EQW Working Papers,* no. WP14. Phila-

delphia: National Center on the Educational Quality of the Workforce, 1993.

Real Jobs for Real People. An Employer's Guide to Youth Apprenticeship. Washington, D.C.: National Alliance of Business, 1992.

Robert Reich. "Education and the Next Economy." Washington, D.C.: National Education Association, Professional Organizational Development/Research Division, 1988.

———. *The Work of Nations: Preparing Ourselves for 21st Century Capitalism.* New York: Knopf, 1991.

J. E. Rosenbaum, D. Stern, J. Agnes, S. Hamilton, S. E. Berryman, and R. Kazis. *Youth Apprenticeship in America: Guidelines for Building an Effective System.* Washington, D.C.: William T. Grant Foundation Commission on Youth and America's Future, 1993.

School to Apprenticeship Handbook. Dearborn, Mich.: Educational Data Systems, 1993.

"School to Work: Transitions that Work." *NEA Today,* December 1992.

Theodore R. Sizer. *Horace's School: Redesigning the American High School.* Boston: Houghton Mifflin, 1992.

What Work Requires of Schools. A SCANS Report for America 2000. Washington, D.C.: The Secretary's Commission on Achieving Necessary Skills, U.S. Department of Labor, 1992.

Work-Based Learning: Training America's Workers. Washington, D.C.: U.S. Department of Labor, Employment and Training Administration, 1989.

Index

AFL-CIO
  Department of Education, 180
  Human Resources Develop-
    ment Institute, 181
  New York State, 182
"AFL-CIO Guidelines on Skill
  Training and School-to-
  Work Transition in the
  1990s and Beyond," 180
Agrarian society, 10, 24
Alexander, Lamar, 57
Alliant Techsystems, 73
Alternative Schools Network, 52
American Dream, 76
American Express, 54
"America's Choice: High Skills
  or Low Wages," 17
"America's Job Disaster," 75
Apprenticeship for Adulthood (Ham-
  ilton), 87
Arkansas
  youth apprenticeships in, 128

Assembly line jobs, 6, 14, 15
Assessment methods, 43
ATM. *See* Automated Teller Ma-
  chine
Austria
  youth apprenticeships in, 85
Automated Teller Machine,
  25
Automation, 102

Bailey, Thomas: *The Double He-
  lix of Education and the Econ-
  omy,* 58–59
Baldor Electric, 101
Barley, Stephen, 6
Bennett, Bill, 143
Bentsen, Lloyd, 94
Berryman, Sue: *The Double He-
  lix of Education and the Econ-
  omy,* 58–59
Bill of Rights, 32
Bither, Eve, 56, 129

Blue-collar workers
  in Japan, 107
  unemployment rate of, 65
Blue Cross and Blue Shield of
    Maine, 37, 142
BMW, 108
Boesky, Ivan, 75
Boston
  youth apprenticeships in, 98,
    128
Bowdoin College, 31
British Isles
  youth training systems in,
    119–122
Brock, William E., 54, 92, 102
Burke, Edmund, 163
Burr, Matt, 99, 149
Bush, George, 12, 40, 41
Bush administration, 92, 94
Business, 60, 79, 92, 102, 153
  low estimation of schools by,
    48–49
  offshoring operations, 195
  opposition to youth apprentice-
    ships, 101, 171
  partnerships with schools, 39,
    88, 96, 135, 198–199
  school reform role of, 8, 83
  trends affecting, 194
  use of technology in, 66, 67
Business-Labor-Education Part-
    nership, 135
  in British Isles, 119–122
  in Denmark, 114–115
  in Germany, 36, 110–113,
    116, 117
  in Ireland, 118–119

  in Japan, 36, 106
  in Maine, 137–146, 157, 158
Business Roundtable Education
    Initiative, 95, 166

California
  education "frameworks" in, 43
  vocational-technical programs
    in, 61
Canada, 191
CDS International, Inc., 167
Center for Learning and Compet-
    itiveness, 167, 169
Center for Strategic and Interna-
    tional Studies, 72
Center for Youth Apprenticeship
    (Maine), 135–137, 143, 149,
    166, 186
"Centers of excellence," 39
Certificate of Core Mastery,
    133
Chamber of Industry and Com-
    merce (Germany), 112
Chamber of Trade and Craft
    (Germany), 112
Champy, James: *Reengineering the
    Corporation,* 17, 23
Chicago, 75–76
Children's Machine, The (Papert),
    55
Chilton Research Service, 47
China, 12
Cities in Schools, 54
Clinton, Bill, 128
Clinton administration, 42, 92
Coalition of Essential Schools,
    50

Cold war, 34
Cole, Paul, 182, 183
Colgate-Palmolive, 23
Columbia Teachers College, 58
Commission on the Common Core of Learning, 148
Commission on the Skills of the American Workforce, 102, 190
Community colleges, 93
Connecticut
  "common core" curricula in, 42–43
Cooperative education programs, 93
Cost-cutting techniques, 4
Cotton gin, 32
Council of Chief State School Officers, 187
Courseware, 57
Craft committees, 138–139, 151
Craftsmanship 2000, 127
Crichton, Michael: *Rising Sun*, 13
Crime
  in United States, 74–77
Cross, Christopher, 95

Daggett, William, 37, 66
  "Future Workplace Is Shocking," 25–26
D & G Machine, 99, 149
Dartmouth College, 31
Deaconess Hospital, 98
Declaration of Independence, 32, 104

Deming, W. Edwards, 43, 61
Denmark
  career preparation in, 110–111
  youth apprenticeships in, 85, 114–115, 130, 167
Department of Education (Ireland), 118
Detroit, 74
Dole, Elizabeth, 92
Double Helix of Education and the Economy, The (Bailey and Berryman), 58–59
Downsizing, 65, 66, 194
Doyle, Frank, 21
Dropouts, 45
  prevention programs for, 153
  reducing, 54
Drug dealing, 74–75

ECS. *See* Education Commission of the States
Education
  American national goals for, 41–42
  continuing, 24
  cooperating with business, 96
  decentralizing, 43
  and economy, 58, 59
  impact of cold war on, 34–35
  reform role of, 8, 60, 89, 144
  standard of living and, 71
  systemic issues underlying, 39, 42, 60–61, 62, 79, 135
  in United States, 5, 7, 31–34, 37, 38
"Education and the Next Economy" (Reich), 15

Education Commission of the States, 42, 48, 49, 50, 60, 62, 129

Education Excellence Partnership, The, 47

Education Summit (1989), 40, 42

Electronic technology, 64

Emple Knitting Mills, 3

Employment crisis
  and crime, 75

Endangered American Dream, The: How to Stop the United States from Becoming a Third World Country and How to Win the Geo-Economic Struggle for Industrial Supremacy (Luttwak), 72

England
  vocational education in, 119
  youth-training programs in, 120, 122

Essential schools, 50

Europe
  productivity rate in, 103
  skilled workforce in, 106, 108
  youth apprenticeships in, 84, 85, 110–126, 153, 167

Executive Council of the AFL-CIO, 180

Farmers, 13, 14

Farrington, Hugh, 69

Fast food industry
  automation technology in, 25

Federal Institute of Vocational Education, 114

Fitzsimmons, John, 114, 126, 129, 137

Flexible manufacturing, 37

Ford, Henry, 14

Ford Motor Company, 33

4-H Clubs, 154

France, 191

"Future Workplace Is Shocking," (Daggett), 25–26

Gateway Assessment test, 130, 132–133, 156

GATT. *See* General Agreement on Tariffs and Trade

GE Bangor, 69, 70

GE Naval and Drive Turbine Systems Department, 69

General Agreement on Tariffs and Trade, 7

General Electric, 21, 26

General Motors, 67

German Marshall Fund of the United States, 108, 167

Germany, 4
  career preparation in, 110, 114
  dual youth apprenticeships in, 85, 108, 111–113, 116, 117, 130, 167
  emerges from World War II, 35–36
  productivity gains in, 191
  schooling levels in, 109
  work-based education in, 110, 114, 197

Gettysburg Address (Lincoln), 32

GI Bill, 34, 150

Index

Glasnost, 13
Global economy
competition in, 4, 64, 126
Globalization, 4, 6, 36
GOALS 2000: Educate America
Act (1994), 42, 169
Goods and services
distinction between, 16, 27
Gorbachev, Mikhail, 13
Gorman, Leon, 22
Government, 60, 79
partnership with schools and
work, 87–88
school reform role of, 8, 38,
39, 83
Governors' Task Force, 130
Graebert, Steve, 69
Grant Thornton survey, 101,
192
Great Depression, 34, 77
Greene, Mickey, 37, 142
Gymnasium, 109, 112

Haarder, Bertel, 115
Hamilton, Stephen, 94
Apprenticeship for Adulthood, 87
Hammer, Michael: *Reengineering
the Corporation,* 17, 23
Hannaford Brothers Company,
68, 69
Harvard University, 95
Hauptschule, 109
Hayward, Gerald, 61
Heald, Anne, 169
Healy, Kevin, 140, 158
Heath Springs, Ltd., 120
Helmsley, Leona, 75

Herbert, Bob, 75
High schools
American graduation rate, 41
education after, 149–151, 193
youth apprenticeship programs
in, 83–87, 98
"High Skills or Low Wages,"
190
Hill's Pet Products, 23
Homicide rates (U.S.), 73–74
Hoser, Albert, 102
Human Resources Development
Institute, AFL-CIO, 181

IBM, 17–20, 56–57
Indirect costs, 18
Industrial jobs, 14
Industrial Revolution, 32, 123,
190, 195
Inner city schools, 45–47, 51–52
Institute on Education and the
Economy, 58
Intelligence added, 16
International Center for Leader-
ship, 26
International Standards Organiza-
tion, 70
International test scores
U.S. students, 49
Inventory management, 37
Ireland
chronic unemployment in, 118
higher education in, 117–119
wages in, 119

JAG. *See* Jobs for America's
Graduates, Inc.

Japan
  education/industry allied in, 106, 107
  emerges from World War II, 36
  lean production in, 15
  productivity rate in, 103, 191
  skilled workforce in, 106
  wages in, 4
  work-based education in, 197
JFF. *See* Jobs for the Future
JMG. *See* Jobs for Maine's Graduates
Job creation
  slowdown of, 3, 65, 68
  technology and, 24
Jobs, 6, 96
  in construction, 84
  downsizing, 65, 66
  fewer, 68, 78, 191
  industrial, 14
  lifetime learning and, 56
  in manufacturing, 84
  offshore shipping of, 64, 78
  professional, 14
  "smart," 68, 69, 79
  technical, 179
  technological nature of, 5, 25, 26
Jobs for America's Graduates, Inc., 52, 108, 129–130, 153, 154, 155, 156, 166, 177, 187
Jobs for Maine's Graduates, 129, 132, 154, 155, 156, 177
Jobs for the Future, 83–84, 85, 102, 166, 171, 174, 181, 186

Jordan, Mary, 51
Jordan, Vernon, 54
Junior Achievement, 186
"Just in time" techniques, 70

Kadamus, James, 55
Keating, Charles, 75
Kentucky, 43
Kok, Jurgen, 141, 199–200
Kolberg, Bill, 92
  Rebuilding America's Workforce, 93
Kozol, Jonathan, 51–52
  Savage Inequalities, 46–47

Labor
  costs, 64
  horizontal divisions of, 194
  and management, 27
  new pattern of, 14, 16
Lackey, Dave, 129
Lean production, 14, 15, 16, 17
Learning
  continual, 19, 23, 24
  interacting with work, 57
  interdisciplinary, 175
  lifetime, 56, 97, 150, 194, 199–200
  on-the-job, 84
  work-based, 94, 152, 163, 169, 174, 179, 196, 197, 198–200
Learning Gap, The (Stevenson and Stigler), 47–48
Lifetime learning, 56, 97, 149, 194, 198, 199

Light bulb, 32
Lincoln, Abraham: Gettysburg
     Address, 32
Linotype machines, 33
Literacy, 45, 98
L. L. Bean, 22–23, 157, 162
Luttwak, Edward, 75
     *The Endangered American
     Dream,* 72

McDonald's, 25, 98
*Machine That Changed the World,
     The* (Womack), 15
"McKernan's Top Ten Lessons
     Learned," 89–91
McLaughlin, Ann, 92
Maine, 78, 89, 128
     "common core" curricula in,
          42–43
     decentralization in, 43
     impact of globalization on, 6,
          69
     layoffs in, 3
     tax revenue drops, 2, 3
     youth apprenticeship program
          in, 99, 129–159, 163, 165,
          177
Maine Department of Education,
     136
Maine Education Assessment,
     43, 133, 145, 156
Maine Medical Center, 99
Maine Occupational Information
     Coordinating Council, 132,
     177
Maine State Board of Education,
     129, 147

Maine Technical College Sys-
     tem, 114, 163
Maine Youth Apprenticeship Pro-
     gram, 130–154, 159, 163,
     177, 199
     basic principles of, 135
     eligibility for, 132
     quality guarantee of, 157
     remedial program in, 156
     student guilds in, 156
     student services liaison within,
          152–155
     and tourist season, 146–147
"Maine's Common Core of
     Learning," 132, 148
Maine's Skills Standards Board,
     199
Manhattan Project, 103
Manufacturing technical asso-
     ciates, 18, 19
Martin, Lynn, 92, 195
Mass manufacturing, 11
MEA. *See* Maine Education As-
     sessment
Mecon Manufacturing, 3
Medieval guilds, 123
Megatrends (Naisbitt), 5
"Meisters," 172, 173, 198
     training of, 136, 142–143, 148
Mexico
     wages in, 3
Michigan
     high-school printing classes,
          33
Middle class, 71
Middle management, 65
Milkin, Michael, 75

Milne, Melissa Morel, 154
Milton Academy, 52
Ministry of International Trade
    and Industry (Japan), 107
Minority students, 51–52
Model T, 32
Modular system, 121–122
MOICC. *See* Maine Occupa-
    tional Information Coordi-
    nating Council
Monotype machine, 33
Morrison, Chip, 129
MTA. *See* Manufacturing techni-
    cal associates

NAFTA. *See* North American
    Free Trade Agreement
Naisbitt, John: *Megatrends,* 5
National Academy Foundation,
    54
National Advisory Commission
    on Work-Based Learning,
    195
National Alliance of Business,
    92, 187
National Association of Manufac-
    turers, 59, 166
National Center for Research in
    Vocational Training, 61, 187
National Center on Education
    and the Economy, 17
National Commission on Excel-
    lence in Education, 38
National Conference of State Leg-
    islatures, 166
National Council for Vocational
    Qualifications, 120

National Education Goals
    (U.S.), 41–42, 53
    1992 Report, 44
    1993 Report, 97–98
National Governors Association,
    166
National Skills Standards Board,
    169
National Youth Apprenticeship
    Initiative, 85
"Nation at Risk, A," 144
"New world order," 12, 13, 79
New York
    crime in, 73–74
New York State AFL-CIO, 182
New York Telephone, 36
Nissan, 107
North American Free Trade
    Agreement, 7
Norway, 191
Novo Nordisk, 115

"O Captain, My Captain,"
    (Whitman), 32
Office of Higher and Continuing
    Education (New York), 55
Oklahoma
    youth apprenticeships in, 127,
    145
Opportunities Awareness, 154
Orr, Jim, 37
Osram Sylvania, 66, 157
Oxford University, 95

Pacific Rim nations
    productivity in, 103

Index

Papert, Seymour: *The Children's Machine,* 55
Parker Hannifin Corporation, 141
Part-time workers, 101
Pennsylvania
  youth apprenticeships in, 127
Performance-based thinking, 43
Peters, Tom: *Thriving on Chaos,* 12
Phonograph, 32
Pierer, Dr. Heinrich von, 195
Portability, 93, 139, 183
Preapprenticeships, 84
Process reengineering, 4
Productivity, 21, 69, 190, 196
  and cost-cutting techniques, 4, 5
  during Industrial Revolution, 190
  in Europe, 102, 103
  in Japan, 103
  and lean production, 15
  microprocessor effect on, 190
  in Pacific Rim nations, 103
  retraining and, 20
  U.S. workers, 3, 65, 96, 103, 191, 192
Programme for Work Experience, 120
Project ProTech, 98, 128
Public schools, 30
  low-income students in, 51

QR Industries, 66–67
Quarterdeck Office Systems, 118, 119

Reagan, Ronald, 90
Reagan administration, 92
Realschule, 109
Rebuilding America's Workforce, (Kolberg), 93
Recession (1990)
  in Maine, 3, 7
Reengineering, 17
  business, 65
  work, 68
Reengineering the Corporation (Champy and Hammer), 17, 23
"Reform networks," 39
"Registered apprenticeships" programs, 84, 182, 183
Reich, Robert, 4, 16, 92
  "Education and the Next Economy," 15
Retention rate, 54
Retraining, 20, 37, 70
Rising Sun (Crichton), 13
Roberts, Edward, 120
Robots, 26, 64, 66, 107
Rufus Deering Lumber, 155

Sainsbury's Supermarket (England), 120
St. Valentine's Day massacre, 76
Sales jobs, 14
Savage Inequalities (Kozol), 46–47
Scandinavia
  youth apprenticeships in, 110–111
Schmidt, Herman, 114
School of Labor Relations, Cornell University, 6

Schools, 5, 82, 92
  "academies" within, 54
  bureaucracy of, 61
  businesses' estimation of, 49
  decentralizing, 43
  essential, 50
  failures of American, 30, 37,
    38, 46, 47, 55, 59, 60, 79
  high, 41, 83
  and industry in Japan, 106
  inner city, 51–52
  linking to workplace, 85–88,
    197
  reducing dropout rate in, 54
  reforming, 83
  suburban, 51–52
School-to-Work Opportunities
  Act of 1994, 169, 181–182
Schultz, Dottie, 140–141
Scotland
  modular training system in,
    121
  vocational training system in,
    119
Scottish Action Plan, 121
Scottish Vocational Education
    Council (SCOTVEC), 121
"Secretary's Commission on
    Achieving Necessary Skills,
    The," 193
Services and goods
  distinction between, 16, 27
70,001, Inc., 53
Sharbonez, Vera, 18, 19, 20
Shorr, Elizabeth, 142
Siemens AG, 195

Siemens Corporation, 102, 117,
    157
Sizer, Theodore, 50
Skills
  academic, 152
  continual learning of, 15, 21,
    23, 56, 97
  employers seek, 151
  and good jobs, 89, 91
  literacy, 45, 101, 192
  portable, 93, 182
  setting standards for, 169, 180
  teaching, 58, 59, 96, 156
  teamwork, 18, 19, 62, 68, 70,
    95, 192
  technological, 4, 5, 26, 27, 68,
    95, 101, 102, 190
  and wages, 17
  workplace, 152
Skills Standards Board, 137, 138
"Smart jobs," 68, 69
Sorbonne, 95
Southern Maine Partnership, 44
Southern Maine Technical Col-
    lege, 135, 136, 151
Southern Regional Education
    Board, 187
Soviet empire
  collapse of, 11, 13
Soychak, Jackie, 146
Space race, 35
Sputnik I, 35
Sputnik II, 35
Standard of living
  education and, 71, 150
  U.S., 65, 73, 192, 193, 195

Index

Statistical process control, 37
Stevenson, Harold: *The Learning Gap*, 47–48
Stigler, James: *The Learning Gap*, 47–48
"Student guilds," 156
Student services liaison, 152–155
Sweden
  apprenticeships in, 116
  career preparation in, 110–111
  productivity in, 191
Sylvania Coil Operations plant, 66

Teachers
  reeducating, 58
Teamwork, 6, 14, 18, 19, 68
  computer-literate, 62
  cross-functional, 22
  production through, 56, 70
Technical institutes, 93
Technical jobs, 14
Technological skills
  electronic, 5
  within German workforce, 4
  within Japanese workforce, 4
  productivity and, 190, 191, 193
Technology, 13, 20, 26, 64
  enhancing productivity, 190
  and impact on jobs, 66, 67, 69, 70
  and job creation, 24
Tech-prep movement, 93
TECs. *See* Training and Enterprise Councils

Terrorism, 74, 77
Thailand
  wages in, 3
Thatcher, Margaret, 119
3M Corporation, 5
Thriving on Chaos (Peters), 12
Timberland Shoe Company, 3, 67
Total quality management, 4, 61, 70
  South Carolina schools use, 43
Tourism
  Maine apprenticeships in, 146–147
Towers Perrin
  1991 survey, 60
Tracking, 99, 100
Training and Enterprise Councils, 120
Truman, Harry, 150
Tulsa Junior College, 127
Tulsa Tech, 127

Underclass, 71
Unemployment, 192
  among all workers, 65
  among young minorities, 52
  in Ireland, 118
  support groups, 66
Unions, 33, 92, 138
  promoting youth apprenticeships, 179–183
United States, 82, 85, 104, 124
  college graduates in, 34
  crime in, 73–77

United States *(continued)*
 education in, 5, 7, 31–34,
  37–38
 falling standard of living, 65,
  71, 72, 73
 Industrial Revolution in, 32
 leading world power, 11
 national education goals in,
  41–42
 1990 recession in, 3
 worker productivity in, 3, 65,
  96, 102, 103, 190, 191
 workforce future in, 21, 196
University of Heidelberg, 95
University of Maine, 129
University of Southern Maine,
  151
University of Tokyo, 95
UNUM, 37, 57, 140, 158
Upward mobility, 76
U.S. Chamber of Commerce,
  166
U.S. Congress, 42
U.S. Constitution, 104
U.S. Department of Education,
  56, 94, 169, 188
U.S. Department of Labor,
  36, 71, 84, 92, 169, 187,
  193

Value added, 16
Vermont
 "common core" curricula in,
  42–43
Vocational Industrial Clubs of
  America (VICA), 154
Vocationalization, 96

Wages
 in China, 4
 in European apprentice pro-
  grams, 113–115, 123, 124
 gaps in, 189
 of Maine youth apprentices,
  142–143
 in Mexico, 3
 in Thailand, 3
 in United States, 3, 102
Wales
 youth apprentices in, 119
Washington, D.C.
 crime in, 74, 75
WAVE, Inc., 53–54
Wendy's, 25
Wescott, Don, 158
Westbrook High School, 149
Wheeler, Tammy, 99
White-collar workers
 unemployment rate of, 65, 66
Whitman, Walt: "O Captain,
  My Captain," 32
Wisconsin
 youth apprenticeships in, 127
Womack, James, 14–15, 16
 *The Machine That Changed the
  World,* 15
Work
 factory, 33
 nature of, 68
 new education for, 77, 98, 99
 new world of, 13, 21–23, 79
 redesign, 4
 reengineering, 68–70
 "shadowing," 109, 111, 139,
  173, 177

"smart," 79
teams, 18
Work, Achievement, Values, and
    Education (WAVE), 53–54
Working poor, 71
World War I, 35
World War II, 34, 191
    Germany emerges from,
        35–36
    Japan emerges from, 36
Wuest, Jack, 52

Yale University, 31
YMCA, 186
"Youth Apprenticeship, Ameri-
    can Style," 94
Youth apprenticeship system for

America, 83, 86, 88, 94, 97,
    98, 100, 102–104, 145, 192,
    193, 195–196, 198–200
    business support of, 171–173
    educator support of, 173–179
    European model of, 85,
        110–124
    parental support of, 183–186
    potential of, 92
    preparation and design of,
        86–87, 164–165, 168–170
    union support of, 179–183
    See also Maine Youth Appren-
        ticeship Program
"Youth guilds," 153
Youth Training Scheme, 119
Yugoslavia, 12